2gether 4ever

2gether 4ever

Never apart. May be in
distance but never at heart.

Roshini Ramakumar

PARTRIDGE
A Penguin Random House Company

To order additional copies of this book, contact
Partridge India
000 800 10062 62
orders.india@partridgepublishing.com

www.partridgepublishing.com/india

Dedication

<u>To my parents:</u>

I always dreamt of writing a book but it became true only because of you both. Thank you so much.

<u>This is for you dad:</u>

No matter where I go

No matter what I become

I can always seek peace by holding your thumb

No matter what I do, No matter how I am

I always get your shoulders for a loud cry and long laughter.

Thank you so much Appa.

Prologue

I wanna go back to my past. Going through the pictures are remembering me the past fun filled days. I did not have any great expectations in my life. All these years I never knew who is friend and who is enemy. But now I can judge. I spoke to everyone here in an artificial way. That's life is that what I learnt. I did many mistakes but it was all never taken on a serious note. But now it does. Mom never expected a call from me, but now she dies if I do not call her. She calls me everyday no matter what. Dad took me on his shoulder, no wonder how heavy I was. But now we never sit together also. Even if I've a big challenge it'll come to an end after I've a scooter ride with my dad. But now we live nearly 3000 kms away. Playing chess with dad, winning in bets, eating ice-cream on a rainy day etc are not there with me now. Mom feeds me parupu sadam (Dhal rice) whenever I hesitated to eat but now I don't even have someone to accompany me to dining hall.

3 months of holidays during school time and almost 80+ friends. All these shows I was never alone. But now I'm almost alone most of the time. Phone calls never gave me the comfort that I got from my loved ones. I craved for love care and affection with no motive.

"When we are left alone we are always left with the past and so I was". **The days which everyone long for –The school life.**

Best Friends Forever

*F*riends uplift the soul. They come into our life to teach us something that we have never learnt before. Getting the friend of our gender will make our life good, but indeed it would be fabulous if we have a friend of the opposite gender. It happens only for a few. That magic happened to me. Ritu, the beautiful chubby girl. That says it all. Everyone would wonder, if I got a friend in my class. But definitely not. I had friends in my class, but none were as close as her.

First day in my new school:

I joined my grade 9 in that school. She was in grade 6. Every one would think how come a girl from grade 6 can become close to a guy in grade 9. But she did. She was very popular among seniors as she was the little champ in school.

By 11.10 am I saw a cute girl standing outside my class, waiting for the teacher to leave the class. After the teacher left the class, she at once entered the class to meet her brother-like friend, Sharvan. Sharvan was the one who gave me company on the first day of school. As she gave him the lunch box, she turned to my side and gave me a look. Oh god what do I call that look as? Was that just a look or an electrifying power?

As I stood near Sharvan, he pointed me to her and said "Ritu look. He is Abhishek", and he added to that I am an NRI (but I was not. It was just to prank her). She turned towards me and lent her hand forward and said "Hi Abhishek Anna (brother). I am Ritu. Welcome to St. Mary's."

"Hi Ritu, nice meeting you". (It might seem so formal but it's that all I could say her).

So Abhi bro, which country are you from?

Eventually by this question I and Sharvan bursted out in laughter. She on a bemused tone asked "what's wrong?"

"Nanum Tamizhan dhan. Avan chumma sonnan". (Even I belong to Tamil Nadu, he was just kidding).

She gave a staring look to Sharvan and turned towards me and smiled.

I wanted to talk to her; but bad luck favoured my side. The bell rang. She waved a bye to us and left to her class.

My mind was completely down after that. Everything in the class seemed out focused. Ritu, Ritu, Ritu, was just the only name that ran in my mind. I wanted to see her again, and talk to her.

It was 04.30 p.m and the bell rang. We departed towards our buses. I and Sharvan took the last seat of the bus. He introduced me to some of the seniors. They without considering me as junior became as close as possible. But I waited for her arrival and nothing more that.

She got into the bus with lollipop in her mouth. I wondered how come a girl can be this beautiful in every aspect. She took the seat before us and immediately turned towards the back seat and offered us a lollipop. I thought she was just to close to my classmates. But she proved me wrong. She was close to my seniors as well. Every one treated her like their own sister. They cared for her, scolded her, appreciated her, and some people even cried for her. I thought if everyone is this close to her, what will be her character? And obviously even I wanted to get close to her.

Luck favored me. We belonged to the same area. So we got down in the same bus stop. We have to walk at least 1 kilo meter to reach our homes. She lived two streets away from my home.

Getting closer:

Every evening we walked together. Though my dad arranged a car for me to reach home from bus stop, I avoided those because I loved walking with her. Days passed. But she called me Anna. Unlike other seniors she called them with their names.

One day while heading towards home she said, "Abhi Anna, I am going for a quiz competition tomorrow. You know what is the first prize? It is the mobile phone with sim card.

Though I felt that I will miss her, I was very happy regarding the first prize. All the best Ritu, smash the first place. (That is the best thing that would ever happen to me).

Ritu: Thank you Anna.

Abhi: Stop being formal Ritu.

Ritu: Huh?

Abhi: Yes, it is been months and still you call me Anna.

Ritu: But Anna I am used to it.

Abhi: Will you stop? Just call me Abhi.

Ritu: Ok, sorry.

Abhi: I am sorry too.

Ritu: That's Ok. Bye. See you the day after.

Abhi: Bye Ritu. All the best.

<u>The Day after:</u>

Morning she did not turn up in the bus. More than her I hope, I was so curious about her result. Not merely for congratulating her but for getting her number. My on way to school was boring as she wasn't in the bus.

Prayer Time:

I had no interest in standing during the assembly
time. After the flag hoisting, pledge, longing advises
and chants by Principal, Correspondent took the stage and
announced about the incidents of previous day.

**"R.Ritu of standard 6 has grabbed the first place in the quiz
conducted by rotary club. She has been awarded with a mobile
and the certificate. I request our Principal to handover the
memento"**

*I was on cloud nine after hearing it. I was overjoyed. I thought
I should give her some gift. What else can I get in school rather
than chocolates? I got some chocolates for her.*

*During interval, she came to my class for showing the mobile
phone. Sharvan wasn't in the class. So indeed she showed me
first. Felt so proud as she showed me first.*

*That evening while walking back home, I gave her chocolates
that I got for her. With a cute smile on her face she said "Thank
you Abhi. You are the first one to gift me something".*

*You are welcome Ritu. I really felt good as she called me without
"Anna" for the first time."*

Ritu, when are you gonna activate your sim?

Abhi final exams are nearing. I don't think I can activate it now.

Why so?

My dad won't let me to.

But Ritu, it's yours. Phone isn't bad as well.

But my dad … ok I'll try convincing him.

Good.

Abhi, do u mind me asking your number?

No. Definitely not. Ask me.

Mr. senior can I get your number please?

Hahaha. Ritu who will mind giving the number to such an cute girl?

9080566778

Easier to memorize. I will give you a call after activating mine. Bye I have to cross the lane.

Bye Ritu.

Text Messaging:

Hi. This is Ritu. (A message popped by middle of night).

Hey Ritu. Dint you sleep yet monkey?

No Abhi. I can use my mobile only after 11. Dad's order.

Oh. That's good. So what are you doing?

Just on bed.

Very good. Then? (The only way to keep conversations going is asking "then").

Abhi, you got Ur exams tmrw ri8? All the best

Thanks dear

Hmm. Don't u miss school?

Yes I do. (In mind more than that I miss you)

Even I miss school. Miss walking with you too.

Even me Ritu. Wish to meet you soon.

In the same way we conversed the every night. I anticipated for 11 pm every night.

One day she suddenly asked me when is Ur bday Abhi?

June16.urs? And y suddenly?

Sept 27. Just to wish you.

I am waiting.

Keep waiting and get ready to see the surprise from Ritu. See you in school tomorrow. Gonna sleep. Goodnight.

The reopening day:

The day I prolonged for is right ahead in front of my eyes. I left to the bus stop 10 minutes before to spend time with her.

Hey Abhi. She came running.

Hi Ritu. You have put on weight.

Oh really? 😞

Hey don't be sad. You look more beautiful than before.

Hahaha. Thank you da.

That made my day. From Anna to da- A good transformation.

We sat on the same seat this time. Never ending chats continued on the entire way up and down.

We got so close. Shared happiness, problems, anger and almost everything. We have thickened the relationship under a single name called "**Friends**".

Being a **good friend** to her is really good. The lie I said myself. To say cheated myself. But I loved her every minute. No matter how close we were but I had no courage to tell her that **I love her**. I was scared of losing her friendship. I tried to dump my feelings. But it burnt out soon as camphor.

The Rumors:

As usual when a boy and girl gets close, rumors and gossips will start spreading. The same happened in our case too. Entire campus was filled with the rumors.

"Abhishek loves Ritu" was the common phrase in everyone's mouth.

Ritu completely avoided me. She never sat with me nor walked with me. I was in the mixed state of emotions. I was happy and sad as well. I was happy that someone somehow conveyed my feelings.

A Week later:

While walking back home, she asked me "Do you love me"?

*I could not tell her **YES**.*

I hid my tears behind my smile and said "No Ritu. It was just a rumor".

She started talking to me normally. That night we spoke in call for the first time. She busted out in laughter thinking about the rumor. I could not control my feelings. I did my biggest mistake in asking her "Don't we make a good pair Ritu"?

Abhi?

Yes Ritu. I am in love with you. Why don't we make the rumor come true?

Stop that. Will you? That's really cheap of you Abhi. Were you the spreader of the rumors? Shut up and good bye.

Ritu listen to me. She hanged up the call.

*We were never like before. I wished and prolonged to talk to her. But it never happened. **I have done the biggest mistake.***

<u>Pain of losing a best friend:</u>

Ritu never spoke to me after that. I tried calling her but she never picked the call. She dint come early to the bus stop and even if she comes she used to stand near the shop (near to the bus stop) and never came near me. In the evenings her mom picked her up from the bus stop. I don't know why all these were happening. I questioned myself "has she hated me completely?" I regretted for the words I uttered that night. Just one question popped up my head "Is that all over between us?" I wished the answer to be NO. But it prolonged to be a YES and nothing more.

<u>June 15:</u>

The day before my birthday. I believed that she will wish me. I thought she was playing with me just to wish me on my birthday. I was a fool.

I waited for her text. But it never popped up in my mobile. In the bus I expected her to wish me but she never turned by my side.

I gave chocolates to everyone in the bus. I waved my chocolate box to her. She neither turned nor wished me. She led me to the peak of anger. I shouted at her "WTF is your problem Ritu?"

Excuse me?

What the hell is wrong with you? Can't you just wish me "Happy Birthday? You know I was a fool waiting for your wishes".

I hope I never asked you to wait. Moreover I don't wish any strange persons. Can you please leave the way? I've to get down.

Strange person? Me?

Yes Anna. Please leave the way.

I just wanted to slap her. But I couldn't. "I love you Ritu". I cried in pain.

Sharvan though being her brother never failed to be my friend.

As of my conscious is concerned it was the first time I cried in front of some people. Those people were supposed to be my close friends. The worst part is they are close to Ritu as well. They can neither console me nor her. They cheered me up and tried to bring me back to normal. Adding to all this, my classmates arranged a party in my class. I was getting normal but still, her words echoed my ears. It was sculpted in my heart.

Days passed. Things changed. In the past six months she grabbed numerous prizes and has become the school's "**Hall of fame**". But as far as I am concerned my condition was getting worse. I went down in studies, lost interest in sports, started boozing and to say "I lost myself".

I texted her happy birthday on September 27. (The last text I sent her). But there wasn't any reply from her. I stopped texting her too.

Board exams were almost near. By the month of January we had our school annual day. Students of grade 7th, 8th, 9th and 10th were clubbed together for Julius Caesar play. Even during practices she never spoke to me. I wanted to talk but I was scared of getting insulted again.

One day during practice, I found her crying. It was the first time I am seeing her with tears. I did not know what was actually wrong with her. But I couldn't withstand her tears. I left the place.

Sharvan was consoling her. He tried his best and brought her back to normal. Later, I enquired him what was wrong with her. He said "she is scared of acting with you Abhi. Nothing else"

Shall I quit from the play?

Hey chuck it buddy. She is good now. She is actually falling for you machi (dude).

I was about to ask the explanation. But then, my practice started. I forgot asking Sharvan regarding it.

Practice and rehearsal continued for the next 10 days. Annual day was a block buster hit. Especially Julius Caesar play was appreciated by everyone. We were awarded with a cash award of Rs.10000. We shared it equally.

After the annual day fun was almost an end and we were cornered to study. Even the friendliest teacher turns strict in the eleventh hour. We had soft skill classes and motivation camp. But saddest part is all these never helped me out. I flopped in my exams. I scored 726/1100.

The only way my motivation camp helped me was it made me decide to continue in the same school. I continued my junior college in the same campus. I chose maths, biology as my major. When I selected this group I had no idea of why I chose it. The only reason I opted it was Sharvan too opted the same.

My last two years in school was at its best. I concentrated more on sports than in studies. I was made the sports captain in grade 12 and Sharvan was the school pupil leader. What else can happen better than this? My team grabbed the rolling trophy that year. Adding to my fate, Ritu was in my team and she helped me a lot in getting the trophy. She, as an individual scored solid 85 points to the team.

When your best friend owns the higher post, school will become your reign as well. Rowdism, strikes, fighting with teachers, beating up juniors and getting suspended from school happened in my life as well.

I kept myself busy. It was just to keep my thoughts away from her. I succeeded in that. I was away from her memories at last.

Time is the best healer, I realized it.

Best feeling in the world is that when you realize you are perfectly happy without the thing that once you needed the most.

It happened in my life. I was perfectly happy without her. Three years passed and she never spoke to me.

Farewell:

*I*t was the day I never wished to arrive. But it was as fast as possible. It was just like a funeral. Everyone was crying. Even I did. All my classmates gathered for the last photograph. I kept it safe for years and years.

We had sorry and thanks session. I apologized to a few and thanked one &only Sharvan. Now, everyone in my class is friends with each other. In the past few years I got many friends. But my first best buddy was no more in my life. It was the last day in the school. She spoke to everyone in my class even cried while seeing a few. But she never spoke to me. I thought I deserved it and remained silent.

After having dinner together with all teachers, friends and juniors we departed towards our home. None had the courage to wave a bye with a smile rather than a tear. Sometimes tears express our love much better than the smile.

While I sat on Sharvan's bike and was about to start. I heard a call "Abhi" I turned back to see who was it. The most beautiful girl I know was right at the back of me. Ritu. She was damn so beautiful. She was like a typical Indian girl dressed herself in saree. The hair that dances due to air and falls in her eye increased my heartbeat. It killed me.

Abhi?

I got out of my thoughts and said "yes Ritu"

I am sorry for everything. I didn't like the way you asked me. It doesn't mean I hated you. After I spoke such, I didn't have courage to see you nor talk to you. I know I have committed a mistake. Will you forgive me? I am really sorry. Do your exams well.

Is that all over Ritu? Can I talk now? I never wanted you to ask sorry. I loved you from bottom of my heart. I was mad about you. I prolonged to talk to you. But those days are over now. You did hurt me a lot, but all this never made me angry on you. I loved you more and more. Please don't be sorry. I have completely forgotten and removed all those thoughts from my heart. Actually, you were right on your point.

But Abhi...

Please Ritu. You needn't feel bad. Let's be good friends. Study well.

You too study well.

Yeah I will. Shall I take a leave?

Ok. Bye. I will miss you.

Ok bye. I wanted to say I'll miss you too but something stopped me from. Call it ego? Might be.

That night when I logged into my fb account I found a friend request. Adding to my surprise it was from was from Ritu. Ritu Rakesh (her full name) wants to be your friend on facebook. Without any second thought I accepted her request. She was online. But I didn't start chatting. After a couple of minutes a chat popped up my screen. It was from her.

Hi. I was scared that you won't accept my request.

Hi. Why not?

Will you forgive me Abhi?

Can we make an agreement?

Regarding?

Please let's not talk about past. Let's start a new friendship from today.

Hmmm

?

Yeah. Ok.

Then what's up?

Just chatting. Wbu?

Just back home.

Where were you?

Hanged out with friends.

Friends? Or friend?

The second one

Hahaha... You and Sharvan are identical twins I suppose.

Hmmm. Might be.

Are you angry on me?

No. Not at all. Why?

The way you talk isn't like before.

Forgot the agreement?

No. I actually wanted you to scold me for this. That's the reason why I spoke about the past.

Hahaha... gone mad?

Yeah I am.

Nice.

But on you.

Huh?

Yes I am mad on you. I am in love with you Abhi right from the Julius Caesar play. I cannot think of my life without you.

Hmm...

What does your hmmmm denote?

Actually I was really happy but I wanted to play with her.

I replied "I was actually waiting for this day Ritu"

I hope you are happy now. ☺

Yeah.

Hmm.

You know Ritu there were days I prolonged for your love, care, friendship etc. But all those are over now. I am perfectly happy without you now. I wanted you to fall for me and feel the pain that I badly underwent.

Abhi please don't do this.

I'm sorry Ritu. Die with my memories.

Abhi. one minute please. (I left offline).

I never thought these words will hurt her so much. She cried the entire night. When a guy is hurt he smokes, boozes, goes for a long ride etc.

But when a girl is hurt all she does is nothing but crying to her death by hugging her teddy bear. Both kills the same way.

I realized how mad I was. My mischievous behavior almost killed her. She cried so much and got wheezing. That night her parents dragged her to the hospital and she was kept in ventilator too.

God!! Why did I do this to her?

Next morning I went and saw her in the hospital. Her parents asked Sharvan to be with her for some time and said they will go home and be back after refreshing.

She was dying to breathe. I was absolutely speechless and so my tears spoke out. All I could do was nothing but sitting near her and catching her hands.

For the first time, I prayed God to give my girl back to me.

Without any further ado, she was getting better. She slowly opened her eyes and saw me. The water storage tank of my eyes got overloaded and started flowing.

She got up from her bed and said "That's okay Abhi. I'll be fine soon".

I hugged her tight and said "I love you so much stupid".

In her innocent accent she asked me "are you cheating me again?"

I started crying so badly. She caught my cheek and said "sorry Abhi. Please don't cry. I am so sorry. I love you."

That evening she was discharged from hospital. I never knew I loved her this much. She did the same to me too. I realized there are two more persons to love me as my parents.

1. **Ritu**
2. **Sharvan.** *I am so blessed.*

<u>*Blooming of love:*</u>

ext morning I was attending online test in study springs and obviously there was a tab opened with face book.

I got a message from her telling Hi. Yeah that was the end of my study hours.

Hi Ritu <3.

What's up?

I was just studying.

Hmm. Sorry if I've disturbed you.

Hey come on. How can I ever think you as a disturbance?

I love you Abhi. I want you to study well and get good marks.

Sure. rituma.

Ritu ma?

Yeah

Hahaha. What have you decided to study?

Physics.

Hey no I didn't ask that.

Then?

Higher studies.

(To be frank it was the first time I thought about my career).

I don't know Ritu.

Don't know? When'll you decide?

No idea. Help me.

Ok tell me the things you love the most.

One and only Ritu.

Idiot. Things. Not persons.

I love bike, long rides, bunjee jump, voyages, travelling in ships, blue sky and SPB's voice.

Nice. So you like travelling right?

Yeah.

You love voyages too. So marine engineering?

Marine? Me? Hahaha.

Yeah. You are perfect for it. Search for information regarding it.

Okay dear. Sure.

Do it right now.

I'll. wait.

Okay.

After 5 minutes:

Rituuuu….

Yes Abhi.

I don't think it'll work out.

Why? What's wrong?

Marine engineering has its scope in north India than in south. I can't stay that far away from you.

Abhi. I don't want your career to be spoiled. I don't want you to stay here and spoil our future. I'll always be with you. I love you.

Ritu. It's really hard you know.

Please Abhi.

Ritu. Let's talk about it later.

No. listen to me.

Will you please stop this Ritu?

Ok sorry.

That's ok.

Ok.

Angry?

No. but I want you to focus on your career.

Ok dear. I'll.

Thank you. Love you.

Love you too.

Ok go and study now. I'll text you morning. Goodnight. Ritu dreams.

Goodnight dear. Abhi dreams.

Every night we had a long chat in face book. She made sure she was right in her duty. She asked me the same set of questions everyday

"How was your day"?

"What did you study"?

"Had supper"?

Though it was so casual and usual, it'll be nice when you hear it from your dear one. She nurtured the inscriptions on my heart telling I've to become a Marine Engineer.

Almost my entire study holidays were coming to an end. I had just two more days for my exams. Stress was crippling up my head. I prepared well too.

Day of examination:

_I_ got nearly 20 calls from my relatives wishing me all the best for the exams. I wondered if I was gonna get married and so these many people are calling and wishing me. I wanted Ritu to wish me first. But she didn't. I went for taking my shower. I have the habit of listening songs while bathing. Suddenly the song on my mobile stopped and a number flashed on my screen. In a disgusted tone I said "Hello".

Hello Abhi. It's Ritu. (In a husky tone).

Haan yes Ritu.

Listen I can't talk for a long time. It's my dad's no. All the best Abhi. Do well. I'll pray for you. Going to temple now. I'll be there till you complete your exams. Love you. Bye.

Ritu.

Yes Abhi. Tell soon.

I love you. Thank you.

I love you too. Ok bye bye. **smooch**.

(A kiss on phone is as alcoholic as getting in reality).

After my shower, there were huge prayers. My mom drew Indian flag on my forehead. My dad gifted me a Parker pen. Grand ma showered her blessings on me.

I reached my exam centre. After seeing my buddies my stress was reduced and we busted out in laughter for everything and nothing. Fun had a stop and the disaster enslaved us. Yes the exam bell. We gathered in the prayer hall. Lots and lots of instructions were passed. Though nothing went inside my mind it was a mandatory to stand there. Our exam halls were dispersed in various nook and corners. Sometimes it's nice not to be with friends during exam times so that you'll not have anyone to confuse you with the answers.

At last my first exam was over. I saw Sharvan sitting on his bike. I believed he must be waiting for me and obviously he did.

Abhi do you have any work at noon? Or can you spend some time with me?

I have never seen him this formal. But I was worried about Ritu. She would be waiting for my message.

Machi (Dude), I am free. But

But?

I need to inform Ritu that I've done well my exam.

Ok fine. You carry on.

That's ok machi. Come let's go.

But Ritu?

I'll take care buddy. Start your vehicle.

Thank you.

Nearest Hotel:

*W*e logged into the next nearby restaurant. He asked me how did I do the exam and I repeated the same question to him. He said it was quite an normal paper for him.

Pointing to a table I said "Machi, come lets seat over there"

No. let's take the third seat.

Already a girl is occupied there. Can't you see it buddy?

Yeah come. He grabbed my hand and pulled me towards her.

He waved a Hi to that girl. Added my surprise, she was my junior, the same class of Ritu. She smiled at me and so I did it back to her.

She was really so nervous and asked Sharvan "why were you this late? Everyone here is looking at me in a bad way." Sharvan caught her hands and said "That's okay. I am sorry."

I was in a bemused state. I wondered if this girl is his sister or girl friend. Why the heck did he call me here? What's happening?

He introduced us to each other. She looked at me and said "Hi Anna".

So I conformed myself that she isn't Sharvan's sister. Abhi I'm in love with her for the past six months. I always wanted to tell you this but time dint favor me.

I really felt bad as he dint tell me in the beginning but later I realized neither I said him about my love in the start. I understood best friend needn't know from the beginning but he should know it first. He also said that Shali is his relative. From bottom of my heart I felt happy for them and believed that there won't be any hindrance in their marriage. I loved talking to them.

By evening 5; we departed home. Sharvan dropped me home. I completed the entire question and answer sessions and rushed to my room. I switched on my computer and logged into fb. I had a message. Obviously it was from Ritu.

Hey Abhi. How did you do?

U der?

What's wrong?

Did you reach home?

R u safe?

I am worried.

Are u angry on me that I hanged up the call so soon?

Were my prayers unanswered?

Was the paper tough?

Did you do it good?

Is everything ok with you?

Why dint you come online?

Pls reply… I'm scared.

Reply soon. My heartbeat is stopping every minute.

I really felt sorry for making her wait this long. I understood the pain she should have undergone as I dint reply. Sorry Ritu.

Hi Ritu.

Hey moron. Where were you?

Sorry. My exam was easy. I had to go out with Sharvan.

You could have said me and left right?

I am sorry. I had to.

Was that so important to me waiting for you?

Hmmm... Yes but no.

What?

As a friend it was important but as a boyfriend it wasn't.

Hmmm ok.

Are you angry?

No. just worried.

Why?

I waited for you this long and so.

Ok. Close your eyes.

Huh? Why?

Do it.

Ok.

Take a deep breath. I'm right at the back of you. Holding your waist, going through your hair, touching your cheek and looking at your grape like lips and biting it. **Smooch**.

Hahaha love you soooo much Abhi.

I love you even more.

Did you refresh after getting back?

No. I know you would be waiting for me. So I thought I'll ping you first.

Ok go. Fresh up. Let's chat at night.

Ok dear ... byeeeeee...

<u>The worst night:</u>

*H*ey Ritu.

Hi da. What's up?

Just thinking of you.

Hahaha. So sweet.

What's up?

Listening songs.

What song?

Teri meri meri Teri prem kahani hi...

Hahaha... nice.

So your meet with Sharvan was planned or accidental?

Accidental monkey.

Why suddenly?

Hmmm. Something confidential with my friend.

Oh ok.

But I don't mind telling you.

Ok tell me.

Do you like Shali?

Which Shali?

Your classmate.

She's shalini. Dare you, call her by the pet name.

Don't be hyper. Do you like her?

Nah. She is an attitude chick.

Hmm, she was good to me.

Huh? What? When?

Today afternoon.

You said you were with Sharvan and now you say you were with her. What's wrong?

Actually both.

Huh?

Yes Sharvan loves her.

Hmmm.

Nothing. happy for them.

Tell me.

Nothing.

Will you shut up and tell me what's wrong?

Actually I shouldn't've been the same to everyone.

What?

Yes. I know Sharvan for the past 10 years and he dint tell me a word. I was a fool telling him everything.

See Ritu. It's not like that. He would have still thought you as a kid.

Ok.

Don't be angry sweetz.

But I am worried.

Hmmm. I'll talk to him.

No need. I'm gonna sleep.

Why?

Not in a good mood Abhi.

Ok sleep well.

Good night da.

Sweet dreams.

I called Sharvan immediately and asked him sorry as he picked the call. When he asked me what was wrong. I explained him how things went wrong with Ritu. Without getting tensed he accepted that Ritu should know it someday or the other and said he'll manage her.

Sharvan called her dad immediately (I stayed on call as well) and said "Uncle its Sharvan here. I wanna talk to Ritu". But Ritu hesitated talking to him. Uncle asked what was wrong between them. He managed telling a small misunderstanding. Sharvan asked uncle if he is at home so that he would go and meet her. But unfortunately, uncle has just stepped out but indeed he gave him permission to go and meet her.

Next minute after uncle hanged up the call Sharvan asked me "Machi can you join me?"

How'll I tell a no to meet her? Come soon buddy. I'll be ready.

It was 9:30 pm and we knocked the door. She was home alone. She came and opened the door with a sad face. Sharvan begged her pardon. I remained silent. She just looked at my eyes. I shook my head and asked her to forgive him.

She said "okay Sharvan. Leave it. I am sorry too". He gave her chocolates and asked her sorry.

"You needn't be sorry Sharvan. I am not putting my nose in your business anymore. You love, you marry. I am not bothered at all. I don't like her that's it."

But Ritu she's so sweet.

Shut up. You cheated me.

Cheated?

Yeah. You addressed her as your sister and now. Cheap of you.

Come on. I was playing with you. Don't you know my serious and funny behavior?

Yes, you were playing and that's what I call as cheating.

Ritu. Please.

Please Sharvan. Let's be like before but don't talk about her to me.

Sorry.

Please Sharvan and she started crying.

I couldn't do anything rather than telling her not to cry. I realized Trust is something that values more than anything in this world. She trusted Sharvan to that extent that she couldn't bare the disappointment he gave her.

We were words less to convince her. We stepped out of her home with a belief that she'll be good soon.

Sharvan was literally crying but he controlled it. I asked him sorry. He said "Machi one day or the other she has to know it. Don't be sorry. Chuck this issue"

Next morning Ritu was so normal to me but not to Sharvan. I felt so guilty for spoiling a beautiful relationship. Sharvan didn't have his smile on his face. He kept thinking of convincing Ritu.

I tried to make Ritu understand but every time she ended up in tears. My efforts were in vain too. You can convince a person who's angry but not the person who cries by getting cheated of over trust.

She called and wished me all the best during my entire exams but she never did all these to Sharvan. Sharvan anticipated her call everyday but she never did.

Days passed and I was doing my final exam. After my final exam my burden was halved and allocated my first job as convincing Ritu and Sharvan.

Sharvan called her dad and asked him if he could come home. Sharvan called me immediately and asked me to get ready to go to Ritu's home. I got ready and waited for his arrival. He arrived in 15 minutes. Even Shali accompanied him. All 3 of us left to Ritu's home.

<u>Ritu's home:</u>

*A*s we entered her home uncle stood up from the couch and said "come in my boy. It's been a long time".

Hi uncle. This is Shali and that's Abhishek. Abhishek is my best friend and Shali is?

Is?

She's my love.

Wow. That's really great. Welcome both of you. Be seated.

Uncle, I need to talk to Ritu.

Actually, what's wrong between you both?

I didn't tell Ritu that I am in love with Shali. She came to know that and bloomed up in the beauty of anger.

Hahaha. I gotta be a lawyer even now I guess.

I wish you stay as a civil lawyer uncle.

Hahaha. Sure Sharvan.

I understood that both her mom and dad are lawyers.

Uncle called "pappu" (her pet name I believe).

She came down the stairs and stood silently behind the couch. Her dad made her sit near and said "pappu listen to me. Sharvan has made a mistake. I accept it's wrong. But learn to forget and forgive things. It is an simple issue and he has come twice to convince you. Doesn't it show how much he loves you? Come on baby. Shake your hands with him"

She slowly stretched her hand towards him and asked "Friends"?

Friends.

Everyone were happy that they've become friends.

Aunty ordered us not to leave home before having lunch.

Ritu said she'll show us the house. After going around the big mahal we reached Ritu's room. It was perfectly a girl's room painted in pink surrounded by teddies and yes it had a huge dressing table and novels too.

I sat near her holding her hands.

Abhi.

Yes Ritu

You are in my room now and soon as a member of my family.

I smiled.

*From beginning till now, Ritu never spoke to Shali nor she did. I asked Ritu to talk to her. She didn't accept at once. She hesitated. As I stared at her she accepted it and started talking to her. It was so formal in the beginning and later they joined together and gossiped about everything. We were very happy seeing them. I relaxed myself telling that the problem **is almost over.***

Lunch:

We all had our seats in the dining table. There were nearly 10-12 items for the lunch itself, which I would have not even had in my entire three meals per day.

Sweet, bean, potato, sambar, rasam, chapathi, dhal, paneer masala, white rice, fried rice and raitha were filled in the dining table. It was like a feast for me. While having lunch uncle turned towards me and asked how have you done your exams Abhishek?

Good uncle.

So what have you planned to do?

Marine engineering.

But isn't it risky in future? Half of year in sea and other half on land?

My throat got struck for a while I cleared it and answered but uncle it's my passion.

Well. But I feel it'll be hard in your martial life. Sorry to be frank.

That's ok uncle.

So what's your dad?

He is a civil engineer uncle owns his own company in Chennai.

Cool. Mom?

She is a govt. school teacher.

Nice. Any siblings?

No uncle.

Good. Good.

I remained silent with a smile. After the same set of questions to shalini, he asked me again

So Mr. Champ are you in love?

*Ritu smiled seeing me. I replied with a **no** to uncle.*

Why not? You look handsome too. Are you not interested?

Nothing such uncle.

Waiting for approval from her side?

Might be.

Answer seems weird.

I remained silent.

Anytime, any help contact me. Even you are like Sharvan to me.

Sure uncle.

After lunch, we were about to bid a bye. Uncle called me alone and said love someone soon buddy. cya."

I was shocked. Is he talking to me by knowing everything or just pulling off my legs?

I reached home and kept thinking the same. I switched on my pc and logged into fb again. Unlike other days Ritu's chat started with

You could have said you love me right?

How can I ever tell that?

Why not?

Ritu they love you so much and won't they feel bad if I say it all of a sudden?

What's there to feel bad?

See I don't have a penny in my hand now. I've to earn, settle in my life after that only I can come and demand his angel.

But, you missed a good chance today.

Chance can be made also Ritu.

Philosophy? Stop it.

Hahaha. Your order, my duty. I'll remain silent.

Lol. Idiot.

Hmmm. What's up?

Just drawing. wbu?

Nothing much.

Hmmm

Ritu, I wanna ask you something.

Yes Abhi.

Do you also wanna become a lawyer like your parents?

Yes. I love the profession.

Nice.

Thank you.

Hmmm. Then?

I am sleepy.

Ok sleep.

Sure?

Yeah.

Abhi.

Yes.

Don't you have anything to tell me?

No. you said you were sleepy.

Hmm ok bye.

Ritu hold on.

Yes.

Wipe your tears.

How do you know?

I may not talk much to you but I know you dear. I am trying my best to change myself. I'll soon match up your expectations. Please don't cry.

No Abhi. You be the way you are. If you change for someone, it'll be like being fake to yourself. So please don't change.

You are one awesome girl Ritu. You deserve my change.

Thank you Abhi.

Love you Ritu. You mean the world to me.

I love you sooooo much Abhi.

Hmmm do you really wanna be a lawyer?

Yes. Why?

Nothing I'll tell you when the time paves the way.

Isn't it a right time?

I don't think so.

Hmm ok.

You don't like arguing?

I love it. But not with you.

Why?

Arguing is all about winning or losing. I prefer losing to you.

But why?

I love you.

I asked you the reason.

I don't know Abhi.

Of all persons you know, why only to me?

I never loved anyone like you or more than you Abhi.

Really?

Yes, I can't think of a day without you. I'll even kick off my bucket if you are not with me.

Ritu. Shut up.

I mean it.

I know.

Will you marry me and stay with me forever?

I promise I'll. I will marry you as soon as I settle in my life.

Hmm. I'll be waiting.

Sure. Go and sleep.

Ok dear. You too sleep.

Goodnite honey.

Sweet dreams.

The entire night I couldn't sleep at all. I kept thinking about her ambition. My family being so orthodox will not accept a girl to work and her profession as lawyer is something impossible for them to accept. How will I convince them?

God please show some mercy on me.

<u>Convincing my parents:</u>

*N*ext morning I just started talking to my mom. I asked her is it possible to do law after maths, bio group.

Yes Abhi it's possible. But it's really hard.

But hard work pays right?

Yes it does. But why are you asking all this?

Simply.

Drop your ideas right now, if you aspire to become a lawyer.

Mom, why?

It is not a profession to withstand Abhi.

Why?

You are a guy and you have no background in becoming a lawyer. Neither your parents nor anyone of your relatives are lawyers. I would've let you study law if you are a girl because there'll be someone to take care of you in the future, but now someday you have to run a family.

So are you okay with a girl being a lawyer?

What's wrong with you Abhi?

Abhi come here, called my dad.

Yes papa.

Come. Sit down.

I was almost nervous, shivering, sweating and almost everything. Is it really hard to tell our parents about someone we love? Yeah obviously it is.

My dad caught my hands and asked "who is that girl Abhi"?

Nothing such dad.

Come on tell me. Think me as your friend.

Sometimes it's hard telling your dad, no matter how close he is to you. I felt that.

Dad.

Abhi I have seen you smiling for no apparent reason, spending so much time on face book rather than spending time with us. I found out you are in love from all this. Listen love is never wrong. But you have to pursue it lifelong.

Hmmm. Dad.

Yes Abhi.

I am in love. Her name is Ritu. Completed 9th. She's gonna be in 10th in no time. She is so good. She can't think of a life without me dad. Neither I can. She'll be perfect for our family daddy.

That's nice. Her family knows?

No papa.

For many years is it going on?

I love her for the past 3 yrs and she loves me for the past 6 months.

What are her parents?

Both are lawyers.

Lawyers? She too wants to be a lawyer?

Yes dad.

There starts the problem. Can you ask her to choose something else?

Dad, I love the way she is. She's so interested in it. How can I tell her not to do?

Will you be okay with her profession? Because even you don't like her profession right?

Yes dad. I don't like. But it's worth adjusting for her.

One last question "will you be happy with her"?

Yes dad I can't think of my happiness with anyone else.

Very good. I trust you Abhi. Go talk to your mom and make her understand.

I am okay with the girl you selected.

Thank you dad.

I sat on the slab in the kitchen and said "Maa I've found a girl who's just like you. She's really good. I love her and so you will. Her name is Ritu.

Stop it Abhi (she left the kitchen).

I went behind her and begged her to listen. The first question she asked me was "Does she belongs to our caste?"

Mom caste is something that doesn't matter in love. She is one awesome girl.

Answer my question first.

No ma. They are Brahmins.

You know our caste right?

Yes ma. But I love her.

What will I answer all our relatives?

They aren't gonna live my life.

Is that so? Ok. Fine. Am I gonna live your life?

Maa. Please.

That girl will be over my dead body Abhi.

Maa listen to me.

Decide whom you want? Me or that girl?

I sat hopeless on the floor. My dad pattered my back and said "She'll be fine soon Abhi. Don't lose hope"

I sent a text to Sharvan telling him to inform Ritu that I'm held up in a problem here and I cannot come online.

Ok machi. What's wrong?

I said my love to my parents. Dad accepted, but mom didn't. Feel so lost da. I don't know what 2 do.

Everything will be fine soon. Shall I come over da?

Yes Sharvan. I badly need you.

He turned up home in the next 20 minutes. I took him to my room and cried badly. He tried consoling me. But it was helpless. How am I gonna convince them was the only thing that ran up my mind. He kept saying "everything will be fine soon Abhi." But those words really had some magic.

Dad kept convincing mom and so Sharvan did to me. We sat together for supper. My mom didn't even see my face. Tears filled my eyes. I left the place.

Abhi.

Yes ma.

Sit. Have your food.

I am not hungry ma.

Abhi. I wanna talk to you. Come and sit down.

Tell me ma.

Bring the girl home. I wanna meet her. You are being so stubborn and this makes me believe that you should've made the perfect choice.

Maa?

Yes. Your happiness is my happiness dear. Bring my daughter-in-law home.

I hugged my mom tight and said "thank you ma. Love you"

Love you too dear. Stay happy. God bless.

Ritu: The girl of my family.

*A*s usual I went to my room and turned on the Pc. Sharvan stayed with me that night. When I logged into fb, Ritu wasn't online. I sent her a message telling her that "maa wants to see you. Tell me when you are free. I'll bring you home"

I hanged on for 15-20 minutes, but there wasn't any reply so I logged out. I and Sharvan spoke for a long time regarding the magic that happened that night. It was perfectly magical. It was 2 am and we forced ourselves to sleep.

Next morning we got up by 9 and as I got up I checked up my face book. I found a message.

Why? What happened? Any problem?

No problem. Everything is going smooth.

Really?

Yes my parents accepted our love and they just wanna meet you.

Really? Wow. Super.

So when are you coming?

I'm scared.

Trust me Ritu. There'll be no issues.

Ok then I'll come today.

Sure?

Yes. Come and pick me up by 11:30

I can't come. I'll send Sharvan to pick you up.

Ok. I'll get ready.

Fine. Bye.

Bye.

At 11:30:

A little angel, almost five feet tall with blue color salwar entered my home. That beautiful girl turned my entire home beautiful from the minute she entered in.

Come in

Hello aunty. Pranams (salutations)

Hello dear. Sit down. Feel comfortable.

What's your name?

Ritu.

Nice. What do you do?

Completed 9th grade aunty. Going to 10th grade from June.

What are your parents?

Both are lawyers.

You wanna be a lawyer as well?

Yes aunty.

What if I tell you we don't accept lawyer girls?

I'll quit my profession.

Why?

Abhi has said a lot about you all. I would love to be with you all rather than with my profession. And it's all nothing when compared to Abhi. But I am forced to study law aunty. I can't get rid of it.

That's sweet of you Ritu. Study well. Settle in life. Let him also settle down. Then if everything goes on well let's think of further steps. But I would love t have you as my daughter-in-law.

Thank you aunty.

You are so beautiful Ritu. My son has taken the best decision in his life.

Abhi come here.

Yes ma.

Don't miss this girl. No matter what happens. Fight for her. Got it?

Sure ma.

Drop her home now.

Bye aunty. Bless me.

My blessings will be always there for you. Study well.

Thank you aunty. Bye.

Bye dear.

Ritu was overwhelmed in joy and she was jumping down the streets. Suddenly she got upset.

What happen Ritu?

Abhi in the next two days you got your results right?

Yes

Will you score well?

I'll Ritu. Don't worry.

Then okay.

Love you Ritu. Shall I hold your hands?

It's road Abhi. But still it's okay. Catch it.

A short walk with your loved one on streets is so immense. It'll stay in your heart forever.

Abhi.

Yes dear.

Will my parents accept?

They seem so friendly and so they'll accept.

Hmmm.

What now?

They always wanted me to marry a lawyer.

It was like a rock thrown on my head. But still I managed telling her to be happy as my parents accepted and said her to brood for the rest later.

I dropped her and walked back home. Mom, dad and everyone were happy with my girl and so I was. Felt like half of my burden is over.

That night as usual I had a normal chat with Ritu. She said she's leaving out of town for the next two days and so she can't come online. Though I was sad thinking of missing her, I wished her a safe trip and asked her to have fun.

The result day:

*W*hile everyone else was tensed about my results I had a sound sleep till 10 am in the morning. Even when they came and woke me up I asked them to stay calm and slept again.

At 11:30 I got up and checked into the website tnresults.in

Register no: 136578

D.o.b:16/6/90

Get results

subject	Practical	theory	Total
Tamil		166	166
English		186	186
physics	50	136	186
Maths		192	192
chemistry	50	147	197
Biology	50	127	177
		Result: PASS	1104

I was so happy with my marks. I copy passed my marks to Ritu in the Fb chat box, took a print out of my marks and left to my school, gave sweets to all teachers and got blessings from them.

The next day, I was searching for the marine colleges in the north. I chose Delhi for my higher studies. The very next day I went to Delhi for my admission and yes I got admission in Delhi marine school without any capitation fees.

The next day I started from Delhi and came back to my hometown.

Ritu has replied to the message. "Happy 4 you and proud of you Abhi."

Thank you. I've joined in Delhi marine school.

Wow. That's nice. When's your college?

June 16.

Hmmm ok.

Hmmm.

Even this bday I can't be with you.

Hmmm yeah.

Started purchasing?

Have to start from tomorrow.

I'll miss you Abhi.

I'll miss you too.

I don't know why I chose Delhi, but even she wanted me to go and look after my career. I believed we'll be in contact but I was back drowned again.

The first sign of depart:

June 2nd:

As I logged into fb, I found a message from Ritu.

"Abhi. I can't text you anymore. Dad asked me to deactivate my account as I'm in10th now. Pls don't be upset. I'll call you often. Take care. Come home before you leave. I love you."

I couldn't even reply to this as she deactivated the profile. Days without Ritu were like the days without me. I had none to chat in fb. I kept it online the entire day just to see if I'll get any message from her. I kept scrolling the entire chat box and kept reading all her messages. I had no-one to ask me if I was good, what I did the entire day or not even someone to ask me what I was doing. I miss you Ritu. My life is so empty without you. Come back soon.

June 13:

It was the day before I departed to Delhi. I went and saw Ritu. I informed aunt and uncle regarding my college and then we (I, Ritu, Sharvan and Shali) went out.

We went out to the nearest restaurant. The chatterbox didn't even open her mouth. She sat near Shali silently and didn't even raise her head to see me. I asked Shali to shift her seat beside Sharvan and I sat near her.

I caught her hands tight and said "Ritu look at me".

She saw me with gush of tears in her eyes.

Ritu what's wrong?

I miss you Abhi and from tomorrow you are gonna be somewhere, where I can't even dream of seeing you. These 10 days without you itself was like living on the other side of hell where I wasn't dead.

But Ritu. You asked me to go right?

Yes Abhi. I'll be good soon. But you know what? I'll miss you idiot.

She hugged me and cried so badly.

That one hour with Ritu is still in my memory. I dropped her home. She raised her hand to wave a bye and she wished me all the best. Her hand was shivering when she shaked it with mine.

Take care Ritu.

You too Abhi.

She ran inside her home. I walked back to my home. Maa was already crying to dad regarding my depart. That night I slept soon to keep myself away from these thoughts.

Hostel:
The pathway to hell:

*N*ext morning Sharvan came home to wave adieu. My mom asked him regarding his college.

PSB college aunty, near four roads.

That's good. All the best Sharvan.

Thanks aunty.

Sharvan hugged me and asked me to take care of myself. All I said him was to take good care of Ritu. Call me whenever you are with her machi. Tell her I don't have so much courage to stay alone there. I need her to be with me at least once in a while. Bye Sharvan.

Bye Abhi. Stay in touch. I'll miss you.

Is going to hostel an hard task? Why everyone were crying? I realized it is. During my entire journey I was lying on my mom's shoulder. She asked me to wash my clothes every now and then, so that I don't've a huge burden. To be frank I never knew how to wash my clothes before that.

I asked my mom "Maa. Anga washing machine irukatha? (Won't there be any washing machine?)

No Abhi. You gotta do everything of your own.

Hmmm. A tear dropped down my eyes.

What happened Abhi? Why are you crying?

Maa I never knew Delhi is so far away from our place.

Just the matter of 6 hours Abhi. Delhi to Coimbatore to Salem.

But I can't come there even during the weekends.

Four years of hard work and then the entire lifetime you are gonna be with me Abhi. Stop crying.

We descended in Delhi airport and headed towards my college. I got admission to my hostel and checked into my room. Mom wasn't allowed inside the hostel and so dad accompanied me.

It was perfectly like a mansion. Cupboards were at most dirtiest, windows were not opening, and fan was running at the speed of 1 even though it was kept at 5.

Dad was undoing my bag. I said him that I'll manage and argued with him telling I'll have my things in the bag itself.

But Abhi. It'll be easy for you if you use this cupboard.

Dad please. I wanna talk to you both now. Anyhow I am gonna be alone from tomorrow. I'll manage.

Another guy entered my room. His name is Rithvik.

Hello I am Abhishek.

Hey I am Rithvik. Where are you from?

Tamilnadu and you?

Agra.

That's nice. Your parents have not come?

No it's my 10th year of hostel life. I am used to it.

Great. cya buddy.

Cya. Bye.

He kept the bags and left the room.

Abhi.

Yes dad.

Abhi you are on your own now. You gotta get up by your own, wash your clothes; adjust with food out here and almost everything. Ma and pa won't be there at the back of you to push you forward. Make sure you complete this with at most desire. A girl is waiting for you there. Do it for her.

Sure daddy.

We have given you everything you asked and now it's the time for you to pave the road for your success.

Ok papa.

Ok beta. Come out. We'll leave to the hotel room now and come and meet you tomorrow.

Dad is there any check-in time in that hotel?

No beta. Why?

Papa. Please spend some time with me. I am feeling so lonely.

Abhi. You are grown up, you shouldn't cry like this. Look at Rithvik how brave is he.

Papa, shall I come and stay with you tonight please?

Abhi.

Please papa.

Ok come let me ask your warden's permission. After continuous efforts of begging the warden, my dad got the permission for taking me with him. I was cuddling my mom the entire night. None of us slept. They kept advising me. But nothing went in my mind. All I could here again and again was "Abhi maa won't be with you from tomorrow". I really don't know why that night went so fast.

From hotel to the college it took nearly 45 minutes to reach. We had some orientations programs. After that I had my lunch with my mom and dad. We roamed about the campus and found my classes for the next day.

It was 5:30 pm and my mom took a gift for me from her handbag.

Advance happy birthday Abhi.

Maa.

Yes Abhi.

First birthday without you.

Yeah beta. I wish it's the first and the last. Open the gift.

It was a Reebok watch. Thank you ma.

Abhi, remember each minute in this watch is your mom's time.

How come?

It is the time I am waiting for you Abhi.

Ok ma.

Take care Abhi. Don't cry. (Hugged me).

Maa I'll be good here. Don't worry.

Dad gave me three thousand rupees and asked me to keep it for my expenses. It is the first time I am getting a bulk amount from my dad.

Abhi here is your tiger balm use it whenever you get headache. Coffee is not available here. Try to manage with tea. Sleep soon daily and call me when you wake up, when you start to college, during lunch after you return back and after dinner also.

Sure ma. Amma if you happen to meet Ritu, tell her to call me.

Sure dear. We have to leave now.

Bye ma. Take care.

(Dad hugs) bye daddy. Take care of maa. Be home soon. She'll find it hard to eat alone.

Sure beta. Bye.

Car left off the gates and I ran back to my room. I was all alone. I unpacked my bags and started arranging it on my shelves. Rithvik didn't even turn back to the room till late in the night.

Loneliness killed me. I went to my dinner alone. Throat choked. Nothing went inside my mouth. Entire home scenario was flashing up my mind. I realized the worth of mom's food. I left to the room and sat idle. My mobile started ringing. It was my mom. I wiped away my tears and picked my call up.

Abhi, we reached Salem. How are you? Is everything set there? Had your supper dear?

Yes ma. Everything good and had supper too.

What did you have?

Chapatti and brinjal gravy ma.

Abhi.

Yes ma.

What did you have for side dish?

They don't offer milk and sugar here ma. So I adjusted with the gravy.

That's good dear. How many did you have?

2.

Why just 2?

Maa my throat was choking. I wasn't able to eat more than that.

You were not crying right?

No ma. I wanna talk to dad.

One minute beta.

Hey Abhi. How are you?

Dad are you away from mom?

Yes beta. Tell me.

Dad I am feeling so low. Nobody is around me except the walls. I am remembering the happenings of home every minute. I just wanna come back to you all daddy.

Abhi, don't make decisions when you are emotional. You might get good friends in college. Take a week's time. Even then if you are not okay come back here.

Ok papa.

Abhi if you stay and brood out there, we can't be happy here as well.

I understand papa.

May almighty shower his blessings on you.

Bye papa. Goodnight.

Abhi. Advance birthday wishes.

Thanks dad.

Sleep beta. Bye

Hmm. Good night pa.

It was 10:30 pm and Rithvik entered the room. I decided to close my eyes tight rather than talking to him. All the stuffs clubbed in my mind. I had no other option than convincing myself.

June 16 12 am:

I picked the call.

Happy birthday machi

Thank you Sharvan.

How's everything?

Hard to take it.

Don't worry buddy. You'll get good soon.

Ok.

Enjoy Mann. Bye.

Bye.

My parents called and wished me. Apart from them, there were none to wish me. They didn't know it was my birthday as well. It was just another day.

First day in college:

*F*irst day in college was very dragging and boring. I just remembered Ritu the entire day. Got some new friends; karthik and ajay. Even they were from Tamilnadu. It was like getting my mouthful of air back.

That evening when I opened my room I got a call from Sharvan.

Hey da.

Stupid. Why was your mobile off from the morning?

I had college buddy. Mobiles aren't allowed in the campus. What happened?

Ritu tried calling you from morning and now she asked me to wish you a happy birthday.

Can I talk to her now?

I don't think so da.

Please man... pleaseeee.

Wait I'll call her.

Conference call connected. This message made my day.

Abhi, happy birthday. How are you?

Thank you Ritu. I'm good.

I called you from 8:30 in the morning but your mobile was switched off.

Sorry dear. How are you?

Abhi when are you coming back?

I've to study here for four years and then I'll be back there for sure.

I miss you ☹

Let's meet by December. I'll be there for sure.

July, August, September, October, November, December. 6 more months?

No other option dear. Keep counting.

Dad's calling. I'll catch you soon Abhi.

Ritu.

Yes Abhi. Tell soon.

I miss you. Can you call me daily please?

Abhi.

Please Ritu.

I'll try calling. If I get caught, everything will be in mess.

Ok be safe.

Bye.

I didn't have courage to wave a bye to her. I spoke to Sharvan for some time and hanged up the call. I went to Ajay and karthik's room and spent some time out there. I was a little out of homesick.

Mom called and asked me how was my birthday?

Birthday was just an day. I missed everyone out there.

Even we missed you dear. You sound a bit good today. Is everything ok?

Yes maa. Got a couple of friends from tamilnadu, it's like being back to normal.

That's really good to hear beta.

Ritu called me ma, she's still crying. Feel so sad for her.

Ouch. She'll be fine soon.

Yes ma. Take care of my girl.

Sure beta. She's actually my girl as well.

Hahhaha. Ok maa. Catch you soon.

Bye beta.

After hanging up the call ajay pattered on my back.

Yes Ajay.

Whose birthday did you mention in the call?

My birthday.

Damn. Today is your birthday?

Yes.

Happy birthday mongoose. We are not eating in hostel mess today. Come let's go to canteen.

Dude I don't have much money with me. Stupid come. We'll pay for you.

<u>No more homesick:</u>

*I*n no time all three of got so closer than before. We bunked classes together, went to the movie together, had food together and almost every day I stayed in his room rather than mine.

Ritu never called me after my birthday. I heard from Sharvan that she is being screwed by her parents as she is grade 10th.

I had the habit of checking Fb daily no matter even if I had no-one to chat with. I re-read all my old conversations from Ritu and smiled like an idiot. When I was going through the chat a message popped up. It was from my girl.

Abhi, how are you? Hope you are not angry on me. Got any new friends? I miss you very badly. I said dad not to arrange any party for me on my birthday. Got dad's number right? Call me on my birthday. Like mess food? Any new girl friends? Dare you don't sight anyone there. Rituma is waiting for you. Love you dear.

Hi Ritu I'm good and you? I am definitely not angry. I heard you are going through a tough time at home. Come on sweetheart enjoy your birthday and send me the pics. I'll call you for sure. Hahaha. Just a few friends in girls and they aren't that *beautiful to look at. Abhi is waiting for you as well. Love you honey.*

Love you love you love you. I was just praying for you to stay online.

I was just re-reading our conversations.

Lovely:-*

Are you safe to chat?

No not really. But I wanna talk to you.

Ritu I got an request to you.

Tell it as an order.

Please don't deactivate, even if you don't come online that's not an issue. I feel like sharing everything with you. So please.

Why are you telling these many please? Order me.

Then don't deactivate your Fb idiot.

As your order hubby.

Jaan.

Hey send me some pics that you snapped in Delhi.

(I sent her nearly 8 pictures)

Wow. You got slim and dark too.

I don't get anything here except chapatti, obviously puts down my weight.

But I'm getting fatter and fatter.

You'll look pretty. Send me your pic.

On my birthday I'll send a special pic for you.

Okay. Two more days. I'll be waiting.

I am dying to talk to you dear.

So I am Ritu.

Love you.

I love you too Ritu.

I gtg.

Hmmm.

I'll be back soon.

Hmmm.

Bye Abhi **smooch** keep this till we chat the next time.

smooch Good night.

Next morning I was fresh and active than ever before. It made my friends turn their eyes towards me. It was the first time I said everyone about my love and everyone were happy hearing it.

The wait is over:

September 27:

I called her by evening 5:30. Spoke to uncle also for some time. I wished Ritu for nearly 15 minutes. Her voice was shivering, choking and almost everything but it was scintillating. I miss you being here Abhi is what she said but in different words. I didn't want her to cry more. I just reminded her about the pics. She promised to send me that night. I thought it's wise to keep the call rather than making her cry.

That night she sent me 16 pics and at last an edited of I and her. We were standing together in the same pic. I kept it as my wallpaper. Then we had a chat quite some time and then she left off for sleeping.

I felt like I got my life back. Nothing was hindering my way. I kept sending her messages everyday and waited for her reply. She replied to the messages once in a while. My heart was less burdened. I loved texting her. Sometimes waiting for a reply is also amazing. I felt that. My heart beat will rise whenever I get a reply from her. For that 5 minutes chat I used to wait for a week or 10 days or sometimes even more. But I had just one satisfaction and that is I'm chatting to her.

Words can't express my love for her. Call it madness? Even more appropriate.

The disaster:

One day I had a beautiful dream and wanted to tell her that. "Jann. You know what I had a dream. We live in a separate place. Everything is well versed out here. Fully furnished house. Just u and I. we are living a happy life together. One day morning you are just running towards me hugging me and telling you are conceived. How happy I was you know? I wish it's a baby girl.

I found that the message was seen and there wasn't any reply. I believed she would have come online for a minute or two. I just kept waiting for her reply and nothing came after that.

What was wrong again?

God please don't make me sad again I want her to be with me throughout my life. I kept waiting for the reply, but I was just asked to wait. People around me asked me to forget her as my semester was nearing. But how can we ever forget a person who's our wallpaper?

I called Sharvan that evening and asked him what was wrong with her? He said he doesn't know and he'll get to know and tell me in an hour.

He called me in next 45 minutes.

"Machi I cannot even see her"

What happen?

Her parents came to know you are in love through your face book messages.

How come da?

Uncle read your messages.

Shit. How is she now?

She is completely house arrested, threatened, and black mailed and even blasted by her parents.

God.

She asked me to tell you not to worry about her and do your exams well.

Machi. How can I?

She also said that she is yours today and forever. She cannot even think of a life without you.

Hmmm. (tears silently flowed down my eyes).

Abhi are you ok?

Haan. yes.

Don't lose hope mapla (dude/buddy).

But Sharvan how'll I convince them.

Ritu will do it for you. Just for you. Don't worry. Just 10 more days. Do your exams well. Let's meet her when you come down here.

Ok da.

Bye man.

Bye Sharvan. Take care.

I completely lost my interest in studies. But friends pestered me to study. I was so irritated then but I was so thankful to them later on. In no time my exams were over. I vacated my room and kept all the stuffs in the locker room. I packed my clothes and almost everything except my bed and buckets.

A way back home:

With two heavy bags, I booked a cab and reached Delhi airport. Boarded on to my flight, I just remembered the day I came to hostel. Catching my maa's hand I didn't even have the courage to face the world but today I am on my own now and I am gonna surprise her. Yes she doesn't know that I'm getting back to town. These 6 months has turned my life upside down. Mom, dad, Ritu are my life but now a person of my life is being caught in a web. How am I gonna rescue her? I had one reason and that's I love her. With all this overwhelming thoughts I reached trichy.

From Trichy it's just two and half hours to reach my hometown. I was happy for coming back to Salem but was really sad thinking about Ritu.

I reached my home. Door was opened. But my mom wasn't shocked seeing me. She instead said "chalo beta! From morning wherever I see, I see you. But you aren't coming these holidays. I miss you"

Maa.

Abhi.

Yes ma.

(She touched me) are you really back?

Yes ma.

She hugged me tight and said welcome beta. How did you come?

By flight till trichy and then by bus.

So sweet. Are you grown up to come alone?

Hahaha. Obviously ma.

Come in. I'll cook everything you like.

Dad came home and was shocked seeing me. We had supper together. Uff! At last it was the supper after 6 months of dinner.

Endless chat all over night, giggles and laughter filled my home after a long time.

Ritu, My girl.

Next morning Sharvan came home and we went to school for seeing Ritu. I got some accessories for her that she'll love the most. After meeting a big bang of teachers I heard a long bell. Yes it was the bell for lunch.

She came out for lunch. She has got pale and weak. The usual smile in her was almost dead. She tried to keep both the side of her lips in opposite direction as soon as her eyes glimpsed me. I just said her "canteen" and left towards the canteen area. In five minutes she came over there. My school canteen is the place where all love birds assemble.

She came near me. I caught her hands. It was damn so hot. Ritu are you ok?

Yes Abhi.

Ritu look at me. (Her eyes were completely red).

What happened?

Just fever.

Why did you come to school idiot?

Because I know you'll be coming.

Are you mad?

I wanted to see you and talk to you Abhi. I'll be fine soon.

I got this for you Ritu.

Thanks Abhi. Abhi, will we get married?

Obviously yes. What doubt is this?

She remained silent for a while and said my parents won't let me to marry you. It'll be very hard to convince them.

I'll do it for you Ritu.

Tears express the purest form of love. That's what happened in her case too. She started crying so much. All I could do was nothing but giving her some faith. She said she wants to talk so much to me and said today is her friend's birthday. She will be going there tonight and asked me to pick her up from there by 6:30 pm.

I went there by 6:15 and waited for her to come. She was sharp there by 6:30. I took her to the farther place from my area and spent an ample time with her. She said she has been forced to stop from all extracurricular activities and she's cornered to study. I asked her marks and even scolded her for scoring low. All she said was she couldn't study as she missed me.

Oh is it? Then I missed you too. Let me not study as well.

No. let us both study good and live well. Deal?

Yeah deal.

Abhi. I've got my smile back after a long time.

I got my life Ritu.

Love you Abhi.

I love you too.

We spoke a lot and lot. I wish the day not to end. Happy to put a smile on your face Ritu.

I almost met her every alternative day. Just a glimpse of her will make my day. I used to wait for hours for that single look. God! She killed me by that look. In the mean time I got my disaster results. Though it was not an disaster I passed with 60%. I then understood semester is all about passing the paper and not about percentage. Though I got a bang of scolding from my parents and Ritu I was actually very happy for my marks.

It was the time for me to get back to hostel but this time I was a bit comfortable than before. Ritu was already down she got worse now. I saw her the day before I left. I advised her to be strong and happy. She said she'll be waiting for the next holidays. Even I wished the same. Will miss you Ritu. I never knew it'll be the last time I saw her.

Back in college:

*S*tarted to my college. Eyes got filled with tears but the lip smiled innocently waving a bye to everyone at home. As I reached my hostel, I felt myself quite normal than the first time. This time I had my room with my friends. What else can be awesome than this? Homesick faded away in a single strike.

As usual college was damn so boring. Longing lectures, getting scolding, acting as if we understood everything was our daily schedule. The major advantage of even semester was that it is the short semester. We'll have exams in 3 months, which means I can get back to my place in 3 months.

March; exam time for Ritu. I was dying to talk to her. Is she studying? Dying in my thoughts? Is she getting scolding? Is she ok?

I prayed for her happiness and hoped and wished nothing was wrong with her.

On her exam day I sent all the best text to Shali and asked her to show Ritu. By 9:40 I got a reply from Ritu "Thank you Abhi. Missing you".

Ritu don't be silly. It's not the time to miss me. Do well your exams. If you are not scoring well, don't ever talk to me.

Hmm sure Abhi. Bye.

I thought being harsh is the only way to make her study. Even she did it.

At last her exams were over. I thought she would talk to me after that. But I truly wonder why all my guesses go wrong? She never turned up online. Then came her results. She scored a way better than I did. She topped the school with 1079/1100. I was truly very happy for her. If there is a doubt of how I came to know her marks. It's obviously from shalini. Even though I was so happy I couldn't express it to her. What can be much worse than not expressing our happiness to our loved ones? To say I didn't have a plural form of it. I couldn't express to my loved one. The one and only one. I was thinking what can I do to make everything good in her life? I actually had no other option than studying and settling in life.

I don't know if luck favored me or if I chose good friends. The only reason I studied was just because of them. When I was turning back to my place I had confidence that I'll meet her somewhere somehow. But even this time my efforts were in vain. I passed by her home nearly 100 times but I couldn't see her. In the morning her house was locked and at night only her parents stayed at home.

When I was bemused with all these thoughts I called Sharvan and asked him to enquire Shalini regarding Ritu. But all said was Ritu never stayed in contact with anyone after her results and she doesn't know where she is.

I tried my best to find her out, but what else can I do rather than enquiring her friends? But she got invisible from her friends. Did she avoid them wontedly or was she pestered to? With all these questions I returned back to college.

It was already 6 months since I spoke/saw her. At a point of time I even got advises from my friends to forget her. Few said she would have forgotten me and few said she has cheated me. I fought with everyone who spoke badly about her.

When I started my 3rd year I had none with me except Ajay. I grew violent and arrogant than ever before. I stopped talking to my parents as even they said me that she's out of my life. How is it possible to forget a person with whom you've spent your entire life with? I've almost lived my life with her. I can't imagine a life without her.

Loneliness has crept up my life. Homesick, lovesick and what not? Finally was hospitalized too. All I wanted was some love and care. Sharvan asked me to talk to my parents. But I hated everyone. I just wanna hold her hands and see her beautiful smile. But where the heck has she gone now?

Parents turned up to Delhi for seeing me, as they realized I wasn't normal. Maa cried seeing me. Even I wanted to cry but I've got that weak that I couldn't even cry. Tears never flowed from my eyes. I wanted my mom to stay with me forever. But I realized that cannot happen.

I stayed with my parents for a week in Delhi and they tried distracting me by visiting many places in Delhi. I couldn't get normal at all. I didn't want my maa and dad to get back to Salem. But they did. I got back to my depression.

I didn't study nor played nor spoke to anyone. I was in a separate world where I just wanted my Ritu.

Was I wrong? Or my life?

I came to my home town after exams. This time I had no reason to stay happy. I stayed at home thinking of Ritu. My holidays were completely out of focus. I got my results. I had an arrear. What was wrong with me? Actually, that was wrong I could not find where I was wrong and hell yeah, Yet again my college starts on 16th June. I left there a day before. I could not sleep at all. I was just thinking many things. I was seeing her pictures and kept comparing my life before few years and now. I wanna go back my past. Going through the pictures are remembering me the past fun filled days. I did not have any great expectations in my life. All these years I never knew who is friend and who is enemy. But now I can judge. I spoke to everyone here in an artificial way. That's life is that what I learnt. I did many mistakes but it was all never taken on a serious note. But now it does. Mom never expected a call from me, but now she dies if I do not call her. She calls me everyday no matter what. Dad took me on his shoulder, no wonder how heavy I was. But now we never sit together also. Even if I've a big challenge it'll come to an end after I've a scooter ride with my dad. But now we live nearly 3000 kms away. Playing chess with dad, winning in bets, eating ice-cream on a rainy day etc are not there with me now. Mom feeds me parupu sadam (Dhal rice) whenever I hesitated to eat but now I don't even have someone to accompany me to dining hall.

3 months of holidays during school time and almost 80+ friends. All these shows I was never alone. But now I'm almost alone most of the time. Phone calls never gave me the comfort that I got from my loved ones. I craved for love care and affection with no motive. I kept craving for it even on my birthday.

The worst that'll happen is when we don't have around us on our birthday. Ritu'll you wish me at least this birthday? It's already since 3 years we spoke. I cried myself to sleep.

On my birthday I would be on my mom's lap when I wake up. When I open my eyes I can the feel the kiss on my forehead wishing me happy birthday. Her face is the first thing I would see. But for the past few years nothing was such. Nothing surrounded me rather than a ceiling fan. I really felt lonely. Missed maa, her lap and almost everything. I tried controlling my tears. I got up from the bed and got ready for the college. I had regular wishes from the persons I know. Rather than wishing me they even asked me how I am staying without my parents and stuffs. I distracted myself from those questions.

While walking towards college from hostel I got my mobile vibrated. I received a text "Abhi, can we talk?"

Sure. Who's this?

You'll know when we talk. Pick the call.

Happy reunion:

My mobile rang and I picked it up

How are you Abhi?

I am good. Please tell me who's this?

Dare you, forgot my voice?

Please tell me who's this?

Happy birthday Abhi.

Thank you so much. But who are you?

My name starts with "R".

Ritu?

Yes Abhi.

Really? Ritu?

Oye. Yes. Why these many doubts?

No I am shocked.

You used to call me Rituma. You proposed me in a call after big bang of rumors in school. I accepted it in farewell. I met you last time during my 10th standard.

Ritu I love you.

Hahaha Abhi. I love you too.

Where have you been these many days idiot?

Sorry Abhi. I was forced to be in hostel. There were no means to contact you. There was just one rupee phone call booth and from there I couldn't reach you at all.

Hmm Ritu. What are you up to now?

I've joined in Indian law school in Bangalore.

Your dream college right?

Yes.

Ritu, shall I call you by evening?

Why?

I'm almost near my class now.

Do you really wanna go?

No.

Then don't.

You sweet devil! Tell me.

How are your studies?

Worst. Got 2 arrears so far.

Why idiot?

I missed you.

It's not the time to miss me. It's the time to study.

Hahaha repeating?

This is the only thing that made me study for the past 2 years.

How's hostel life? Everything set?

No. but I am happy.

Why?

I can talk to you everyday right?

Hmmm.

You know there were times I even lost my heart and tried suicide, but the only thing I kept telling myself is Abhi is waiting for you.

Why stupid?

Homesick, bad friends and your memories.

Happens. It was for your good.

Hmmm. How are aunt and uncle? I missed them too.

They are good. Wanna talk?

Yes.

Hold on. I'll call them.

As I called them, my mom got shocked and picked it up telling "Beta is everything ok?"

Maa I am good. There's a special VIP waiting to talk to you.

(Conference call connected).

Aunty.

Ritu dear. How are you?

I am good aunty. How are you?

I am good too dear. I can now understand the source of laughter in Abhi's voice.

Hahaha. How's uncle?

He's fine dear.

(All regular questions were going on track).

My mom said "okay Ritu. You both talk. I'll call you both later".

We continued talking. She again scored a way better than I did. She scored 1136/1200 and even topped in CLAT exams. I felt very proud of her.

I asked about her parents. She started crying. She cried in pain telling they are still the same way Abhi. They changed so much. But as I dint talk to you for these two years, they believe that we are separated.

Hmmm.

Are you ok Abhi?

I am just thinking of convincing them.

Everything will get on well.

I wish so.

Then we kept talking about gossips regarding our school. I had the best birthday ever. From morning 10 am -5pm we were just talking.

In the evening, my friends arranged for a party. I really enjoyed it to core. Ran the entire hostel to get rid of the birthday bumps. But I can't get rid of it. I got it badly. My legs and hands started paining so much. I texted her telling "I am gonna sleep honey. Tired".

Ok dear. Happy birthday.

She was the last one to wish me. I slept very happily.

Possessiveness — the outcome of real care.

*N*ext morning I sent her "Good morning". She replied me have a nice day after wakes up. We kept it as a regular habit. Evening as I come back, we used exchange texting and start talking for at least 30mins/day. We shared everything that happened on the entire day.

I was little worried about her friends. It's been two months and she had no proper friends. She is a little reserved too. She likes people who behave properly to her. She never spoke to any guys out there as she was scared I would scold her. Obviously I'll. But for her comfort I asked her to mingle with everyone.

From next day, she did mingle with everyone. She roamed out with her friends even after college hours. We hardly spent time for us.

I was happy for her. (The lie I said myself).

She called me regularly and spoke but it was not like before. I couldn't express how I felt. I love her and she's only mine. Call it possessiveness? I don't mind.

It was the weekend. She called me in a happier tone.

Yes Ritu, tell me what's so special?

How did you find out?

I'm not like you to go through others feeling just like that.

Huh? What does it mean?

It means nothing. Tell me what's up with you?

Nothing much. Tomorrow is my friend's birthday and I am gonna bunk my class for the first time.

Ok.

What reaction is this?

Whose birthday?

Arnav's birthday.

Ok.

Abhi. Tell me what's wrong with you?

Don't ask me anything. You decided to go right? Go for it.

I'm telling you right?

Yes. Just informing.

Abhi you wanted me to be happy and so I mingled with everyone.

You avoided me.

Avoided you? No.

Yes, whenever you called me I was dull and you dint even realize it.

I asked you. You said you were tired.

This is the way you understood me.

Abhi, I believed you wouldn't have any problem with it.

In what sense did you decide that?

Please Abhi. I am sorry.

See I am no way different from other guys. I love you and I am damn so possessive on you.

Abhi, I love you too.

I know that Ritu. But I don't like you hanging out with them often.

Hmmm. I have to. When I am in Rome I gotta be a roman.

But Ritu be careful with guys. I don't want you to be in trouble.

In trouble? Or you don't want anyone to propose me?

Actually both.

Hahaha... Abhi you could have told me before itself right?

I thought you would realize it.

I did.

Huh? Then why did you react such?

I actually wanted you to scold me.

Stupid.

I just wanna die hearing all this Abhi.

Hahaha. I'll kill you after marriage.

Lol. Why so?

I was just kidding. I'll die if you leave me.

Don't talk such idiot.

You mean everything to me Ritu.

So you are to me.

We argued, quarreled, fought, and never understood other's course, But these were the simple things that would separate us. But there were numerous things under a single word "LOVE" that united us.

I had my final semester. I've to join work after that. I went to my hometown. Ritu didn't have holidays that time. I decided to climb on to Bangalore for a day.

Bangalore trip:

*O*ne of the most memorable trips. Started by 6 and reached there by around 9 or 9:30. Within these 3 hours, we stopped nearly 5-6 times only for eating.

Oh yes, we denotes myself and Sharvan. On the entire way I kept asking him "how'll be Ritu now?" I used to imagine and suddenly ask him "machi she must be grown up right?"

Hey Abhi. Will you zip your mouth Mann? You are asking me the same question for past one and half hours and how do I know it mapla? Even I didn't see her.

Yeah right?

Yeah.

But buddy, she'll be grown up right?

Hey shut up man.

No. you tell me.

Hey for god and heaven sake will you stop it?

I tortured him to that extent that, he lost his patience and drove damn too fast. As I entered the campus, I got over excited and asked the security the way to girl's hostel. I had to fill up so many forms and formalities before I could meet her.

Her warden called her up. She came with a 3/4th pant and a t shirt with a towel in her head. I suppose she has just showered.

Pointing to me her warden asked "who is he?"

Mam, he is my brother.

(A mini heart attack passed by me).

Is it?

Yes mam.

They have come to take you out. You may go.

Thank you ma'am.

She looked at me and said "Anna. Two minutes. I'll dress up and come."

I laughed but suddenly I got into a doubt that if she had really forgotten me? In the clumsy thoughts, it was so dreamy with a chill breeze, while trees were wavering, while leaves were shredding appeared a beautiful angel dressed in white and black. Her free floating hair passing through her face was *simply amazing. She asked me to sign as her brother and in the next 15 minutes we left the college.*

I and Ritu took the back seat of the car. Poor Sharvan was made the driver.

For the first few minutes, we were just talking. All she asked me was "how did you come Abhi. I never expected it from you". I observed her so much. She was not like before. The girl who never stopped talking is so matured now and uses so nice words when she talks. It's obviously nice to see her such. But I didn't like it. Rather than finding faults, I thought I should enjoy with her.

I caught her hand. I understood how protected she felt when I did it.

Abhi, are you angry on me?

For what?

For talking to guys.

No dear.

Then what made you to take this long to catch my hands?

Were you expecting it?

Yes.

Ritu, how much will you make me to fall for you?

Hahaha.

Please don't smile.

Why?

Don't.

Tell me.

Your lips are adding my curiosity.

She smiled gently and in the next two seconds her smile reached her eyes. I turned to the other side. She pulled my head and forced me to see her.

Ritu, leave me. You are killing me. I need some oxygen now.

I'll give you.

smooch

In the next two second, her lips were on mine. I got the perfect oxygen.

We got down in the nearest hotel. Adding to our fate I saw my aunt and uncle out there. They asked me "Abhi. What are you doing here?"

Aunty (as I passed). She turned to Ritu and asked "You are Ritu Rakesh right?"

Yes mam. How are you?

I am good. Thank you. Abhishek, Ritu is my student. How do you know her?

We studied in the same school aunty.

Okay okay. Take this visiting card. Both of you come home.

Aunty, he is Sharvan. My friend.

Nice meeting you Sharvan. You too join them.

Sure aunty.

I banged Ritu for not telling my aunt is her teacher. She innocently asked me "How do I know she's your aunt?"

Sharvan asked us to stop fighting and asked us to find a solution. I called my mom immediately and said her regarding the things that happened. She asked to me to reveal the truth to them. I got some confidence and decided to go to their home.

We enquired the way to the local persons and set our way towards their home. It took two hours to reach their place.

We had all casual talks and suddenly my uncle asked me "How are the chicks in Delhi?"

Uncle?

I mean the girls.

Good uncle.

Just good?

I don't find anyone to love there uncle.

So it means you found someone here?

Uncle.

Yes Abhi.

Yeah uncle. I've found.

So are you in love?

For the past 6 years.

What? From your grade 10?

Yes uncle.

So who's my daughter in law?

That girl is with me.

Filmic? You are gonna tell that she's in your heart?

No uncle.

Then?

It's Ritu.

(After a minute of silence) uncle said "Really? Perfect choice Abhi."

Welcome to our family Ritu.

Thank you uncle.

So both of your parents know? Asked my aunty.

My parents know, they accepted. Her parents knows as well, but.

But?

They want us to be separated.

God. How are you gonna manage?

There is ample of time aunty. She still has 3 years course.

Just three years dear. Leave that. Ritu who's your local guardian?

None mam.

Shall I help you?

Mam?

Yes, add me as your local guardian. I'll help you in coming out of hostel every weekend.

Mam. Really?

Yes dear. You are supposed to be my daughter in law in few years' right?

Yes mam.

Then call me aunty.

Sure aunty.

Ritu blushed in happiness for getting a new family. So I was. I really felt happy for the way my aunt and uncle behaved with Ritu. She has become the angel of not only my family but my aunt's family too. Who could hate this girl? Obviously no-one.

We went out for dinner and had so much fun. My aunt's daughter became so close to Ritu. I just kept capturing my angel through my eyes. Nothing can be better than this. But all this had an end when we dropped her in the hostel. My aunt filled up the guardians form. Sharvan uncle and my cousin left us alone.

Abhi, thank you.

Thank you?

For surprising me, for hugging me, for giving me some oxygen and for giving me a guardian.

You deserve it Ritu.

We were happy the entire day. But now it's really hard to wave a bye to her. But that is what I should do now.

Bye Ritu (the only word I could say her)

Abhi, don't leave me here please. (She started crying)

You got to study here Ritu. I'll come and see you before I start to Delhi. I promise.

I hope those fake words consoled her. She believed it and asked me to leave. She ran inside the hostel. It was like going to the past. She did the same way when I left to Delhi. Time is too fast.

I started from Bangalore. Aunt, uncle and my cousin left their way home. I kept texting her. In an hour she was normal. She started mingling with her friends. I dint visit her before I started as I promised. Obviously, promises are meant to be broken. Actually I dint want her to cry. That's the main reason why I dint meet her.

Everything was sound and smooth between us. We never fought, but I always had an insecure feeling about Ritu. It was just because of Arnav. Ritu tried to avoid him. But he never stopped talking to her. I asked Ritu to be safe with Arnav but all she said me was "He is like my brother Abhi". But I was damn sure that he's flirting at her. I believed that Ritu'll know her limits. I remained silent. I didn't feel that she'll leave me and go but I felt that she'll be in trouble for no apparent reason.

She avoided telling me about Arnav. I believed she didn't wanna tense me up. She kept visiting my aunt often. In a short span of time she has become the darling of my aunt's family.

She had her final exams. On the last day of her exams they (she and her friends) decided to hang out and get on boards to their hometown.

I didn't stop Ritu from that. I asked her "Is Arnav joining too?"

Yes was her reply.

Ok Ritu. Call me when you start from college and once you board to Salem.

The next morning I called and wished her all the best and reminded her to call me when she starts from college.

By around 12:30 pm she called me and said she has done her exam well and she has started from hostel packing all her stuffs. I heard a huge noise around her. All it said was "Ritu come fast".

Abhi, shall I call you a bit later? Everyone is shouting here.

Ok.

Talk properly Abhi.

You go first.

Abhi.

Stop Ritu.

Why are you angry now?

You are asking me (voice started again)

Abhi. Tell me.

You are asking me to wait for you just for their voice and not stopping them from shouting right.

Abhi, you'll understand but whereas they won't.

Fine.

Abhi, if you be like this I cannot be happy.

Then do something to make me happy.

Abhi, I'll give you silently. Take **smooch**

Thank you honey.

I love you Abhi. Call you soon.

Take care. Bye.

Bye.

I started doing my work. I kept seeing my mobile. How beautiful you are Ritu! I just love you so much.

<u>The unexpected day:</u>

*I*t was nearly 2 pm and she called me. She said she'll be starting only by 6. I thought she would have started early. Thinking of all this I picked the call up.

Yes Ritu. (There wasn't any reply).

Ritu?

Abhi. (In a crying tone).

Hey is everything ok?

No.

Ritu please don't cry. Tell me what happened.

(She continued crying)

Ritu, are you there? Are you okay?

Abhi, scold me first.

Scold you? For what?

Do it first.

Failed in exams? You have just completed your exams right?

Stop kidding Abhi.

Please tell me.

Arnav proposed me.

(I wanted to break his teeth from the minute she said it. I managed acting so decent. But that stray dogs life is right over is that what I felt).

Ritu come on. It's all common in a girl's life. Just tell him you are in love with me and move on. What's the use of crying now?

I said him.

Then leave it. He'll move on by himself.

He didn't.

What?

He tried to behave in a wrong way.

Ritu. Are you safe?

I slapped him.

Good. Then why are you crying now?

He scolded me as bad as possible.

What the fuck did he tell?

He called me a "Bitch". (She started crying badly).

Ritu please don't cry. Give me his number, I'll take care.

No Abhi. Please.

Will you just shut up and give me his number?

OK.

Give me.

I'll text you.

You are texting me.

Okay.

Who's near you now?

Swetha.

Give her the phone.

I asked Swetha to take care of Ritu and convince her. She promised me to do so.

A message popped up on my screen with his number. I didn't call him immediately. I waited for Ritu to board on to bus. As she called and said me that she has started to Salem, the next call I did was to Arnav.

A voice said hello.

Hello Mr. Arnav?

Yes who's this?

I am Abhishek.

Abhishek?

Ritu's boy friend.

Oh, hi.

What did you call Ritu as? You called her a "bitch"? I hope you got more influence of the word from your family?

Shut up Mann!

You mind your tongue first. One more time if you cross her way, you are a dead meat for sure.

But what's your problem dude? I love her. Are you feeling insecure?

Shut that ass. I don't mind you proposing her. I know about my Ritu. You moron called her in a bad way and you want me to fuck my ass and sit here?

(He remained silent).

Hello?

I am sorry Mr. Abhishek. I understand how truly you love her. God bless you both. I won't interfere anymore.

Thank you and sorry for being harsh.

That's ok. I'll apologize to Ritu.

That's indeed not needed. I'll convey her. Bye

Bye.

Arnav never came in her path after that. I said her to be careful and advised not to trust anyone. She nodded her head for everything but I wished something went into her head. Actually, she took all my words seriously. She never spoke a word to him after that. This made me so comfortable than ever before.

Holidays:

Ritu was very happy during her holidays. Her dad and mom were back to her as before. They never scolded her. She has become the apple of their eyes. But all these were based on the reason that they believed that we were totally out of contact. Ritu never exposed like talking to me. She avoided texting me when she was with them.

Every night I spoke to her. Sometimes her mom enters the room. She manages telling her that she's listening to song and sometimes she also said she's talking to her friend Abhinaya.

Ritu is that kind of girl who hesitates to speak lies. But after she loved me she hesitated to speak the truth. She believed that lies will spoil all kind of relationship. But why did you change such Ritu? I am sorry for changing you.

My first voyage:

*S*he left to hostel and I was about to set up my first sea journey. Ritu will be all alone is what the only thing that ran in my mind.

The before night I called Ritu. She seemed brave.

Ritu I've to leave tomorrow. I'll call you once in two days. It'll take a week for me to reach Brazil. You will be fine right?

(Clearing her throat) Yes Abhi. I'll be. All the best.

Ritu keep yourself busy for two days. Go to my aunt's home. Keep concentrating on your studies.

Hmm ok Abhi. You take care. Take first aid with you. It's your first voyage. You may fall sick.

Ok Ritu.

Sleep soon. You gotta get up early right?

Yes.

Sleep then.

I am starting by midnight 2. Shall I call you that time?

No Abhi. Text me.

Why?

Because (clearing her throat again) I don't wanna cry when you start.

Take care Ritu. (My eyes became watery)

Bye Abhi.

Bye dear.

I've stayed 3 years without talking to her, but it wasn't as worst as this. While I was about to start I texted my mom first

"Maa take care. I'm starting now. I'll be back soon"

There wasn't any reply from her. I believed that she should have slept. Next I started typing my text for Ritu. My hand was badly shivering.

"Ritu I am gonna start. I know it'll be hard for you to take it. I promised to call you once in two days. But I don't know if I can talk for a long time. After reaching Brazil I'll have desk work only. I'll call you daily from there. Please take care of yourself. All these are just for 3 more years. After that you can sail with me as well. I love you."

I kept my mobile aside and waited for the command to start.

A message popped up "I think I shouldn't have suggested you this course. Anyhow I'll be waiting Abhi. You too take care. I'll miss you. Be safe. Once when you feel giddy or something take rest. You are more important to me. Love you too"

I had no courage to reply to that. I switched off my mobile and started on my voyage. Everyone will be so excited about their first experience. But I wished it to be last. I can just make one call through satellite connection and that too only once in two days. I thought I'll call my mom and ask her to inform Ritu rather than calling Ritu and asking her to inform my mom.

Maa kept asking me the same questions. "Did you eat beta?" "How are you?" and usual stuffs. The food was much worse than in my hostel mess, but I couldn't tell her. I said her food was good. I want my mom to be satisfied with a feeling that I'm good.

I badly regretted for disappointing Ritu. But I had no other choice. After landing in harbor, the first thing I did was calling Ritu.

She was very happy as I called her. I promised her that I'll call her in a couple of hours. I then called my mom and informed her that I'm safe.

I reached the place where I was supposed to stay. After refreshing myself I called Ritu. We spoke nearly for two hours. I said my entire happening in my voyage to her. She said she has got her results and she has passed the first year with 7.4 cgpa. I asked her to concentrate more in her studies and she assured that she will.

First salary:

I stayed in Brazil for a month and started again on my voyage. I reached Delhi in one month. My 6 months of voyage at last had an end. I took leave for 10 days and left to my hometown.

I gave my first salary to my parents and got their blessings. Giving first salary to our parents is the most memorable thing. Smile on their face is what that makes our day.

I got a salwar for Ritu in my first salary and headed towards Bangalore for meeting her. I gave her the salwar and she was very happy seeing it. She promised to keep it forever. We went to her college food court and ordered veg. burger.

Ritu said "Abhi. I badly want to have Tamilnadu Sāmbhar."

I smiled.

Why are you smiling?

When I was in Brazil I didn't even get Indian foods to eat.

Then what you had?

Sea foods.

Sea foods? Fish?

Crab and prawns as well.

Aaah. Stop that.

You still didn't start eating non-veg?

No.

Super.

Arnav came inside the food court. Abhi don't turn all of a sudden, that blue shirt is Arnav.

Oh really? One minute.

Hey where are you going??

I brought Arnav to our table.

Ritu introduced me to Arnav. Arnav he is Abhishek, my…

Yes I know Ritu. We have spoken before.

Oh that's nice.

You both make a good pair.

Hey thanks Mann.

Wanna have something? Would you like to?

Hey that's okay. You guys carry on. Bye.

Cya buddy.

Abhishek you are really a stupid.

Ritu. Come on it was just for fun.

I spent some time with her and left Bangalore. Her holiday's starts from the next day I started from her college.

How fast these years have passed by? She has completed her 3rd year and I've gone for 14 voyages. But things were still the same. She cried badly when I started. No matter how old we grew, we can never stay away from each other.

Once I had my voyage during her birthday. It was the worst time ever. She cried so badly. I felt damn so lonely in my entire voyage. "When we are left alone, we are left with the past". It's obviously true. I felt very bad for not wishing Ritu. She would have felt damn so bad. Sometimes I wondered how she will be without me after our marriage. Then I compromised myself telling she would sail with me.

But will she give up her profession? But even if she does what's the use and necessity for her to do so? She has studied hard for all these years. Will her parents accept? What if it becomes a problem in future? Let this all be apart, first of all can I stay without her for 6 months, if she decides to practice law? Definitely no. After landing on the end of my voyage I informed Ritu and maa that I'm safe. I said I'll call them after reaching my place.

Even before refreshing myself I called Sharvan. Sometimes a friend may not help you in getting out of the problem but you need to tell them because you wish to. I kept asking him all the questions that crossed my mind. He listened to everything with utmost patience and finally said me "Machi you are telling a single phase in 100 ways".

What?

Yeah you can't live without Ritu right?

Yeah.

Then do something for it.

Hmm.

Did you talk to Ritu?

No. Have you wished Ritu on her birthday?

No machi.

So get ready to be banged Sharvan.

I actually called her 10 times buddy. She didn't pick up. She'll be banged to me this time.

What? Really?

Yes Mann!

Ok. I'll talk to her.

Ok buddy. Bye take care of yourself dude. See you soon.

Bye Sharvan.

I spoke to mom for some time and then dialed up Ritu.

Hello.

Ritu.

Haan, yes Abhi.

What's up?

Just back from college.

Hmm are you tired?

No Abhi.

Belated birthday wishes Ritu. I know this will bring you tears but I had no connectivity that day.

Abhi, you needn't explain all this. I know you would have missed me the entire day. I wish it doesn't happen to me.

I don't get you.

I can bear if you don't wish me but I can't take it if I don't wish you.

Hmm.

Abhi?

Yes.

What happen?

Just thinking.

About what?

How lucky am I Ritu? I got you, my parents who accepted my wish and does everything for me. You all even control your emotions for my sake.

It's because of you Abhi. You make us special.

Okay chuck that. How was your birthday?

I didn't celebrate.

What?

I neither picked any calls nor went out of the room that day.

Why idiot?

I thought it'll be nice to celebrate after your wish.

Sorry Ritu.

Hey come on. Let's celebrate it to together after couple of years.

Hmmm. What about your law then?

Abhi.

Don't you like your profession?

I do.

Then how can you sail with me?

I don't like it more than you.

Ritu, shall I call you later?

Why?

Please.

Okay carry on. Bye.

I kept the call and started thinking. What did I do to the girl who has done everything for me? Nothing. People can't leave out their aspirations. Even as a child we won't give up the doll or chocolate to anyone. But this girl is ready to give up her career? God, what shall I do to her? The only thing I could do was giving up my job and do higher studies.

I chose Ms-Ocean technology. It is a crash course available only Abroad. I chose NUS. Ritu was at the end of 4ᵗʰ year. Before I started from India I asked Ritu to talk to her parents regarding our love. She hesitated. I gave her some strength and asked her to talk. She accepted it and said she'll do it during holidays.

Days in NUS:

With a hope that everything will get on well, I left to Singapore. Days in Singapore were not easy at all. My work burden was heavy. I didn't get any good friends. I hated loneliness but it loved me more. I couldn't talk much to Ritu as she was at home. I texted her regularly.

On a fine morning, Ritu was showing her mom all her college photos. I messaged her "I miss you honey". A message popped up on her screen telling "A message received: Abhi". She called me immediately and said "Abhinaya I am with my mom now. I'll call you later".

She called me in half an hour and said "Sorry da. Mom was near".

Did you talk to mom?

No.

I asked you to. Remember?

But I could not.

Why?

Whenever I think I should start something or the other stops me.

Do you think we have so much of time?

No. just a year.

Do you wanna prolong/extend it?

No.

Then you gotta talk to them.

But.

See Ritu; just don't piss me, if you wanna live happily with your parents blessings. Go talk to them or else I've no issues.

(She remained silent).

Hello?

I don't have courage as you think.

What should I do now?

You come back to India let's talk together.

Let's have the engagement that time.

Abhi, I want you to be with me.

How is it possible?

Stay on line. I'll talk to them.

Now?

No. I'll call you when I talk.

Hmmm. Ok.

Okay Abhi, I'll call you later.

More than her, I was nervoused. I prayed for her parents' acceptance. But what would be interesting if everything happens as we wish?

She called me in sometime. I even thought not to pick up. But I did.

Her dad asked "Ritu, we are planning to see matrimonial stuffs for you. What do you say?

Dad, no.

Why dear? Gonna pursue higher studies?

No.

Then?

Dad I don't know how are you gonna take this.

Ritu, please don't tell me you are in love.

Dad (she remained silent)

I am sorry.

Ritu?

I am in love.

What?

Yes daddy, I guess he'll be perfect for me.

Shut up. Will you?

Dad listen to me. (He left the place)

Ritu relax. Tell me who is it. Our caste?

Maa its Abhishek. I am in love with him for the past 7 years. He is someone I can't forget at all.

Ritu enough. You know what caste he belongs to right? And us? Nobody will accept it. Better forget him.

Mom I can't.

Then forget us.

I had no idea of how to convince Ritu. I truly felt strange of her parent's reaction. I asked her not to worry and said that they'll accept soon. But neither I nor she had confidence in it. But having faith is human nature.

When people in abroad fall in love all they need is other person's acceptance. But in India:

1. *Girls parents must agree and so as boys parents should.*
2. *Her relatives and his relatives must accept.*
3. *More than that both the caste must coincide.*
4. *Apart from all these their horoscope must also match.*

How stupid? But we have to call it as tradition. I thought they'll listen to her words. But they didn't. Tragedies added up my life. I had practical sessions two days after this problem. I need to go on a voyage to read about the equipments. I informed Ritu regarding it but she became damn as worried as her parents were seeing matrimony stuffs in a fast mode. I believed that nothing will get worst in a day. But it got worse than I could even think off.

Her parents brought a guy to their home and even black mailed her to accept. Her part is just shaking her head when her parents ask her acceptance. She tried talking about our love to the guy, but he didn't even mind to take it as a big deal and accepted to marry her. She begged her mom to stop it but they didn't accept it. Her mom threatened that she would die if Ritu is not accepting. Engagement was taking place in her home.

Poor girl, she called me 120 times and my mobile was out of coverage area. Even without knowing what to do, she decided to end her life. I called her after reaching my room. Nobody picked it up. I called Sharvan immediately and asked him check out what was wrong. He went to her home and learnt from the servant that she's hospitalized. He rushed there immediately and asked her parents. They said him that she has cut her vein and she's in critical stage.

Sharvan called me and said all this. Words didn't turn up in my mouth. A silent tear rolled out from my eyes thinking that she's dying again because of me. I asked him to take care of her and said I'll be there in a couple of days. As I said I left to my town in a couple of days.

I heard she was getting better. I went to the hospital to meet her. I was thrashed away by her parents. I tried my best but lost. I left to my home and cried badly to my parents. More than me, they were worried.

I went to the hospital everyday but all I had was insult. They didn't let me to see her also. Third day when I went to the hospital, I came to know that she was discharged. I always had a shoulder to cry. Guess its mom's? No. It's my dad's shoulder. My mom was nearby me, crying even more.

In this situation what'll all parents say? Definitely to give up. But my dad said "Abhi, your tears must have some value right? Go fight for her. You deserve her and nothing more than her."

Papa?

Yes beta. But this time you are not going alone. We are joining you.

Though I accepted it, I didn't want them to get insulted. But they dint mind getting insulted for me.

We went to her house and the first success was they called us in rather than pushing us out. My dad started talking to her dad. Her dad cried and begged to leave his daughter. All he said was his prestige is important to him, and he can't face his relatives if his girl marries a guy of different caste. He begged us to leave. We can fight with a person who screams with hatred but not with the person who cries out of love. We left the place with no sign of happiness. I had a stock of water in my eyes which hesitated to flow in front of my parents.

I called Sharvan and asked him to come home. I explained him those that happened. He dialed Ritu's number from his mobile and asked me to talk to her. I cried literally. She asked me to be *patient for a day or two and promised me that she'll sort out this entire problem. Her parents didn't even talk to her. Her mom at least advised her to forget me but her dad didn't even turn to her.*

Untiring efforts of Ritu:

*S*he called me after two days and said "I am talking to my dad now. Stay on line".

Dad.

Yes Ritu.

Dad I need to talk to you.

Tell me.

What's your problem dad?

Ritu.

Yes. Tell me.

Nothing.

You are not talking to me, you dint even call me for food, neither said me goodnight.

Ritu.

You have hated me papa.

No dear.

Dad, you always paved a way for my wish. Dint you?

I did.

But why not for this?

Ritu please talk to me anything rather than this.

I wanna talk to you dad.

I don't like him. That's it.

You don't like him or his caste?

Actually both.

Tell me one reason why you hate him? I'll tell you 100 reasons to love him.

He smokes, he drinks.

Do you know for whom he did all this?

No.

He did it because of me.

Ritu, he is of different caste and you are gonna put down my head for sure.

Dad your prestige is important to my life?

Ritu, you'll be happy with the guy I see for you. Trust me.

But whatever he does, it'll be like Abhishek doing to me.

Ritu.

Dad, stop shouting. I won't marry anyone rather than Abhishek. I love him papa. I can't think of anyone in my life. You claim that I am putting your heads down, but if something happens to me after marriage don't feel guilty. People will scold you more then than now.

Blackmailing?

No dad, telling you the truth.

Ritu, I won't accept it.

I won't accept any guy. I'll keep doing the same.

Stop it.

Dad I am craving for my happiness and shaping my life for the future. Please understand.

(She started crying badly).

Her dad convinced her and said "give me some time to think Ritu"

Ok papa. I'll wait in my room.

She came to my room and said "Abhi, did you listen?"

Yes. Sorry.

Sorry?

Yes Ritu. You are facing so many problems because of me.

I'm facing problems to live with you. Don't be silly. I wish they agree soon.

I know you are facing so many problems because of our relationship. But I promise you just one thing Ritu I'll never let you worry after our wedding.

I know Abhi. Your course is over?

Got final exams.

You need to go back?

No. online exams.

Then what about job? No sailing?

No.

Why?

Simply. I may get job in Singapore or Malaysian harbors.

Wow.

Keep me updated of the things happening there.

Sure Abhi.

Had your tablets?

No.

Go have it.

Ok.

Call me as per your dad's reaction.

Sure.

Bye honey.

Bye sweetheart.

Her dad seemed to get convinced whereas her mom kept polluting her dad. Things were getting good one day and the next day it was vice versa. There was nothing improving. It was in the neutral mode. Nothing was going ahead. She begged, cried and even blackmailed. They accepted for a day and denied the next.

Melting of stony heart:

*R*itu made her last attempt. *Dad, I am leaving next Monday. I just have 3 more months to complete my course.*

Ok Ritu. I'll arrange car for you to leave to Bangalore.

Papa, what have you decided?

Regarding what?

My love.

Ritu, tell me just one thing. What will you do if he goes on voyage for 6 months?

He is trying ocean technician job. He needn't sail after that.

It is not available in India right?

Yes dad, he's trying in Singapore.

Hmmm.

Dad?

Can you stay that far away from me?

Dad he'll be there for me as you are.

You mean he'll equify me?

I mean he'll substitute you.

Hahaha...

Dad I love him but definitely not more than you. I'll drain when I leave you and go, but I'm sure he'll make me good. I can't live without you paa. Even if I marry him without your interest, I'll run back to you in two days begging your pardon.

Ritu what if I don't accept?

I'll wait. Even I didn't love Abhi initially, the same way I'm sure you'll also like him.

I'll talk to his parents.

Dad?

Yes Ritu. I'll. I value your feelings.

Thank you so much daddy.

Her dad called my dad in an hour. He asked sorry for his behavior and asked permission if he could come home for further proceedings. My dad readily accepted it and we were all on cloud nine.

Her parents came home the next day and asked for my horoscope and gave Ritu's. I asked my parents not to see horoscope and even they don't believe in all these. But her family lives in it.

This time we were in over confidence that everything was going on smooth. Fate laughed at us and said everything is not that easy buddy. You gotta face a lot more.

Yeah when we were about to reach the destiny, roads were worst than before. Horoscope didn't match. Adding to that the astrologer also said that it'll affect bride groom's life if the girl marries him. Now everyone accepted our marriage, but horoscope didn't.

How many hindrances can a person cross? Parents, caste and now the horoscope. But it meant so much than anything else. Though my parents don't believe, they'll obviously take a step back when it comes to my life. Ritu has set out to college. I had no courage in compromising her parents. Obviously I succeeded in compromising mine. Ritu gave me a biggest job to be done. It's nothing else than compromising her parents.

Best thing I did in my life:

I went to her home in two days time. I stood at the doorstep and hesitated to go in. Uncle saw me standing out called me inside and asked me to take my seat. Aunty was very casual and even offered me a drink and biscuits.

Abhishek how is your ocean technology?

Going good uncle.

Completed?

Exams are commencing on Monday.

Job?

Got job in sea shine Marine Corporation.

Singapore?

No uncle. In Malaysia.

Good.

Uncle, Can I tell you something?

Yes Abhishek.

Uncle, I understand you believe in horoscope and you are scared that it'll spoil my life. (I badly started sweating, uncle caught my hand. It gave me so much of comfort). Uncle all I can request you is to trust me and believe me more than those 12 boxes. From your point of view all your fears are valid. No matter even if I don't live with Ritu for a long time, I just don't wanna die without her. A tear rolled down my cheeks.

Uncle wiped it away and asked "when are your exams getting over?"

October 2ⁿᵈ uncle.

Can you wait till November to take my angel as your princess?

Uncle?

Yes. Let's have engagement during November.

Thank you so much uncle.

My Ritu has made the best choice.

Thanks uncle.

We'll come to your home next week after you complete your exams.

Sure uncle. I'll leave now.

Bye Abhishek. Take care.

Bye uncle, bless me.

God bless you beta.

I left to my home and started jumping in joy. I called Ritu and said her about all this. She was over excited and said this is the best thing that can ever happen to her. After having my complete happy talk with her, I took out my books and started studying.

In a week's time I've completed my exams and I've done it really well. Her parents came home and finalized the engagement date. It was on November 7th.

<u>The most awaited incident:</u>

*M*y 10 years of wait and Ritu's 8 years was just right in front of us. We had a gala time. Engagement took place for nearly 5 hours. We decided to have the utmost celebration.

The priest read the invitation.

"Raghuram and Meera's son Abhishek is marrying Rakesh and Reena's daughter Ritu on July 26. May god bless them both with fullest of happiness, wealth and prosperity".

Best things in life are felt with the closed eyes than with the opened eyes. I closed my eyes when priest read it. God, it was mind blowing. We needn't edit pics like being together. We snapped a lot and lot of pics being together.

We had the best part of our life after the engagement. I left to Malaysia for my job and Ritu was in her lapse of last six months. We kept counting the days for our wedding.

Yearning for love is a better feel than enjoying it.

Days passed away fast than we expected. Ritu left Bangalore once for all. She reached Salem on June 7th. There were only one and half months for our wedding. She purchased all her clothes and kept snapping it and sending me on whatsapp. I loved her selection. But every time she wasn't perfect in selecting. I even scolded her for not selecting a good one. She rushes to the store immediately and exchanges it with something even better. Invitations were under printing process and selecting the invitation was the most difficult job.

June 16:

My last bachelor birthday. Days were in a fast forward mode. Days flew. I had the happiest birthday. Wishes poured on my birthday. I was counting my days. It was just in a flying mode.

It was July 15 and I landed in India. I underwent my shopping and completed in a couple of days. Life can no way be better than this. Spiritual stuffs started from 20th. Ritu was prohibited from coming out of her home.

Relatives filled up in my home and so in Ritu's place. The happiness of my parents were boosting up day by day. But I badly felt bad for Ritu's parents. Will they have the same smile on their face? Yes, but definitely an artificial one. I wished to meet uncle.

<u>Day before wedding:</u>

The day before wedding I went and saw uncle. I went to his home and I found him sitting alone in the office room. I knocked the door. Wiping away his tears uncle asked me "Abhi is everything ok?"

Uncle I wanna talk to you.

Tell me Abhishek.

Uncle I can understand how you feel now. I can realize why you are sitting alone. The reason is Ritu right? Sometimes I used to wonder if I can ever love her as you do. I know I can't. But trust me uncle I'll take good care of her. I know you'll miss her so much and your home will be completely empty without her. But uncle, I'll bring her very soon to meet you. Don't worry uncle. Don't think she's gonna be a homemaker after doing five years of hard work. I'll make sure that she pursues her higher education there. I don't have any problem in that. I'll be proud in saying that my wife is a lawyer. Uncle at last I just wanna tell you one thing. I am really sorry for taking away your happiness and thanks for showing such a beautiful girl to me. I just want one thing from you "Trust me". I'll definitely take good care of her. I'll try to compensate you.

Uncle hugged me and said thank you Abhi.

Thanks to you for making my dream true uncle.

I left home and I was feeling a bit light hearted. I don't know if uncle was better now, but I felt happy for doing my duty. As I entered home my mobile got vibrated. I received a text from Ritu.

"10 years of untiring efforts is right ahead in 16 hours"

I replied with ☺

Can we talk?

Yes.

I kept talking to Ritu the entire night. I was so nervous than ever before. First question that popped up in my mind was "Will I take good care of her?" More than a question I guess it's my responsibility to do so. With all these fears I even had dysentery that night.

From Ritu Rakesh to Ritu Abhishek is a great burden of joy overloaded on my head. She took it so happily. But it added fear in my nerves. I promised myself that I'll take good care of Mr. Rakesh's princess.

Ritu this is the last day I'm talking to my sweet lady love. Tomorrow we'll be unofficially married and from the day after its official.

Dum boo. It's already 1 am.

Really?

Yes.

Happy marriage life sweet heart.

To you too dear.

Be ready to change your second name darling.

I already live in it Abhi.

We spoke for nearly 30 more minutes and kept the call. She sent me all the things she's gonna wear on Sangeeth and enquired me the final clarification of if it'll suit her. I loved her innocence and texted her patiently till her doubts were sorted off.

I wasn't able to sleep the entire night. Was it because of extreme happiness or extreme fear? No matter what it is, I tortured Sharvan with the same set of questions.

1. *Machi will I keep her happy?*
2. *Will she be happy with me?*

3. *Will I fulfill her wishes?*
4. *Will I be a good hubby?*
5. *Will I compensate her dad?*

Sharvan got extremely pissed off. He said "will you shut up and sleep? Else I am leaving the room". Ok Mann! Relax let's sleep.

Sangeeth:

_W_e dressed ourselves like north Indians. Games, fun and laughter filled the entire hall. My friends asked me to propose her, sing a song for her and even asked me to lift her up and reveal her weight. When fun was overflowing my friends decided to put an end to it. Fun at last had an end and people started talking about us.

Few people advised us to adjust with each other and asked one of us to walk away if the other is angry. All these will seem very common to those who's in love for almost a decade. It felt the same way to me. I just wanted to hear from two persons.

1. Sharvan
2. Ritu's dad

I invited Arnav also to our wedding. He took his chance in speaking. He came to the stage hugged me first and said "Buddy I need to tell you this. You both look damn fabulous together. May god bless you both. I truly feel happy for not following Ritu after you spoke to me. You wanna know why? It's because I am sure I wouldn't have fought as you did and before that she wouldn't loved me as well. True love these days are hard to find. You both have got one for each other. Please flourish and nourish it". The guy I hated to core is speaking well about us. It's all because of Ritu.

From those two persons, one person took the mike. I stepped a bit forward from my seat and waited eagerly for him to start. Sharvan started "I am really sorry Abhi, I am your friend but today I am talking in favor of Ritu."

I shook my head and asked him to carry on

Ritu is my sister right from the school days. But now, she is the bride. Some things are really hard to digest. The same way even this is being so hard to me. I still can't think her more than a school girl. But she's grown up now. If someone asks to tell me a perfect sister the only girl that will pop up in my mind is Ritu. If someone asks me to tell a perfect daughter I'll tell the same name. She has been a perfect daughter, sister and from tomorrow a perfect wife as well. Can anyone stay the same all throughout the life? But she did. I truly wonder how a girl can be the same way for almost all these years. I really brooded badly when she cried in pain. But I didn't show all those to her because I felt my duty is putting the smile back on her face. If Ritu wouldn't have loved Abhishek I would been in the first phase along with her parents in seeing a bridegroom for her. Rather than a duty it'll be a responsibility for me. A note to Abhi's family: You all think she is so sweet, but she is a crazy devil. She argues to everyone except you people. It means she has already started adjusting even before you started thinking of the word called "adjusting". Please take good care of her." Sharvan was already very emotional and when he said the last line tears started flowing away "Abhi, she was a wonderful daughter, perfect student and a best sister and from now an ideal wife and whatever sacrifices you make for her is everything she deserves. You cannot find any other girl like her Abhi. Please take good care."

Ritu was already in overwhelming tears. She thanked him for the beautiful words. I couldn't do anything rather than going and hugging him.

People around us even advised us how to take care of the child, how to save the money and lots more. They were very serious in what they said, but it ended up funny from my perspective.

Ritu's dad was the last one to talk. He started saying that "I'll try not turning up emotional and I'll take a lot of time to complete please do bear with me."

"Son-in-law, I thought I'll start by addressing you as the new family of my daughter. But I think it'll be inappropriate because in no time she is gonna get married. You are the family for her. Believe me I don't have a problem in that. I, in fact want my daughter to have you as her priority. Now it's the time for us to take a back seat in her life. We would happily accept it. But I've one request to you-"please keep her happy."

I am more than sure that you'll keep her happy and perhaps she'll be more happier with you than she was with me. But like other fathers I obsess on my daughter's happiness and so it makes me say again-please keep her happy. She never was and she'll be a burden for me. She's in fact the reason why I smile and breathe. I am getting her married because this is what nature of law demands. I am helpless in the face of culture and therefore I am sending her to her home. She was the happiness of my home and now she'll light up yours. I'm giving my world to you please make sure it remains beautiful. I am giving away my angel please keep her as your princess. I've raised her up with blood and sweat and now she's wonderfully perfect. If at times if you feel that my angel has done or said something wrong feel free to scold her but handle with love she's very fragile. If at times she feels low be with her, she needs some attention. If at time she cooks badly please do bear it. It's our mistake we never showed her the kitchen. If she falls sick please show her some care and make her eat because my angel will skip her food. Care is the best medicine for her. If she fails her responsibility please chastise her but empathise with her she is still learning. I don't mind if I don't see her for years, I don't mind if I don't talk to her daily. I'll be more happy if she doesn't remember me much and even if she does please adjust with her.

She remembers me because of the love I showed her. It's not her mistake though. My only motive is my daughter's happiness. It's in your hands now.

Dear son in law, these words needn't mean much to you, but if you are blessed to be a father of a daughter someday, you will appreciate them better when each piece of your heart shouts- please keep her happy."

Ritu started crying so badly and left the stage and hugged uncle. Even I had gush of tears in my eyes.

"Thank you so much uncle and I promise I'll take good care of her. I don't know what else to say."

I convinced Ritu for some time and brought her smile back. Dance and fun continued. At last people asked me and Ritu dance as well. After having our dinner we departed to our rooms. In the extreme tiredness I slept as soon as I went to room.

<u>The most awaited day:</u>

*E*arly morning it was 4:30 and my mom woke me up. It was the first time I was seeing that time. After having a great shower I dressed myself as per tradition. Dhoti was really very difficult to wear. After wearing dhoti the first thing I did was practicing myself to sit and stand with it. I succeeded in that. Next thing I rehearsed was tying the nuptial knots. Laughter filled my dressing room.

There came the time to leave the room. I cannot express my state of mind. Was I over joyed? Or extremely nervous? To say both.

Ritu was obviously damn so gorgeous. Traditional stuffs prolonged for 30 minutes. One of the most important traditions was changing Ritu to my caste from her caste. It was really hard for her parents to take it. They had tears and obviously with a smile. After that we had Kasi yatra-The funniest part of the marriage. In this, I have to act like going to Varanasi as I hate the life out here. On the way, the girl's parents will come and offer me the girl and beg me not to go there. The funniest thing is even before Ritu's parents begged me out I accepted it and asked them to give her daughter. Everyone around laughed like mad. I couldn't bear the traditions of Brahmins marriage. Ritu's dad even washed my leg considering me as lord Vishnu. I begged uncle not to do all this. But he asked me to remain silent and said all these are compulsory. Then, came the important time in my life. Yes the "Dum Dum Dum". Ritu sat on her Dad's lap". I tied those three knots.

"One soul, two hearts, three knots".

Ritu's mom was already crying. Everyone congratulated us and I made my first official kiss on Ritu's forehead. Whistles and applauses followed it.

"True marriages begin when we love the one we marry and they blossom when we marry the one we love".

After continuous rituals for an hour we came down the stage and had lots and lots of fun.

The depart:

I had to leave to Malaysia the next week after wedding. In that one week's time we had feast in almost all the relatives home. Ritu was very normal that time. She didn't even think about going away from her parents. But the day before leaving India she was extremely dull.

She was packing her stuffs. I just went and sat near her and asked "Ritu is everything ok?"

Abhishek I'll be fine.

I caught her hands and said "Don't worry Ritu. Everything will get on well"

I will miss my family so much. But as dad said this is what nature of law demands. I know I'll be happy with you but when I realize that my parents won't be there from tomorrow I couldn't bear it. Please tolerate with me. I'll cry for some time.

She started crying badly. I didn't compromise her. I felt that her parents deserve these tears.

Next day in the airport I hugged uncle and said "Thank you uncle".

Abhi one minute.

Yes uncle.

I always wished to have a son but Ritu compensated all those. But now even she's leaving us, we will be desperate in her memories. You asked me to have faith in you and yes I do have a lot of faith on you. With all those can I ask you something in return?

Definitely yes uncle.

Will you be my son Abhi? Will you do the honor?

Sure appa.

I hugged uncle again. Sorry my second dad. Ritu was crying so badly and she felt it so hard to wave a bye to them. From now Ritu Rakesh is Ritu Abhishek. Even in the flight ticket it was printed such.

I just felt how strange the life is? Ritu has become the daughter of my family and I've become the son of her's and we have two parents to love us even more.

Epilogue

I know you are facing so many problems because of our relationship. But I promise you just one thing Ritu I'll never let you worry after our wedding- **I kept up my promise. The first promise that I followed without breaking**

True relationships don't mean that there won't be any fights, but it's all about how soon we bounce back to normal. The same way I and Ritu had lots and lots of fights but at the end of the day we love each other even more. We hated each other's profession but we learnt a lot about other's work to make ourselves better.

Ritu completed her ACS and she works for an MNC. Each and every day we fell more in love with each other. There were numerous problems that ruined us down. But we were united by a common name and faith. "THE LOVE". It kept us alive and happy. Love needn't be perfect; it just needs to be true. We followed it. We were true to each other. No matter even if the truth was bitter and brought us hell lots of fights. We spoke only the truth.

In a short span of time we were blessed with a baby girl. We named her Tania Abhishek. I understood the words of uncle much better now.